Kamado Joe Grill C 2022

By Carl Duca

CONTENTS

INTRODUCTION

Basic Grilling Guide

These basics will help you learn how to grill. Remember to always follow a few rules:

Keep your grill grate clean to prevent sticking.

Give yourself plenty of time to prepare and heat up the grill before cooking.

Always keep an eye on what you're grilling.

Do not use spray bottles of water to control flare-ups, as this will only make the fire worse. Flare-ups are caused by too much fat and too much heat. Trim excess fat from any meat you plan to cook beforehand, and when you flip the meat, move it to a different part of the grill so as to spread out the fat drips.

Have the proper grill tools to do the job.

Oil the food, not the grill. Oil burns away at high temperatures so it is pointless to oil the cooking grate.

Spice your food at least an hour before you grill to allow the flavor to sink in.

Do not add sugary sauces or marinades to meat on the grill since this causes burning over open flame.

Place grilled food on a clean plate, specifically when cooking raw meat.

Keep your grill away from anything flammable like lighter fluid, fences, your house, etc.

Charcoal Grilling

Charcoal grilling is much more an art form compared to gas grilling. It gives you a more authentic grilled flavor and cookout experience, but it isn't as convenient or predictable as cooking on a gas grill. With a charcoal grill, no matter how expensive or fancy it is, there is no temperature control valve. You control the heat by the way you build a fire, how you adjust the vents, and how you good you are at keeping the lid on. It does require more learning and mastery, however, it is just as versatile as a gas grill. Charcoal grills can reach temperatures above 700 F or maintain temperatures around 200 F. You can sear a steak and still

4

cook low and slow. Many charcoal grills even have rotisserie options.

Preparing for Charcoal Grilling

Successful charcoal grilling requires more than just the grill and the charcoal. There are several factors to keep in mind when charcoal grilling.

- Keep the charcoal grill clean; ashes and debris block vents and make fire control difficult.
- Make sure the vents work; rusted or corroded vents are hard to adjust.
- Own a pair of fireproof gloves. Charcoal grilling requires you to touch hot things; be prepared.
- Have a charcoal starter to help light charcoal or use a charcoal chimney.
- Put the grill in a safe place where it cannot be knocked over.
- Keep grilling tools close by.
- Have a good stick or grill tool nearby to move burning coals around inside the grill.
- Practice. Charcoal grilling takes time to master but is worth it.

Building a Charcoal Fire

It takes practice to build a charcoal fire. A few tips will help you get started:

- Light the charcoal, then spread it to build your fire.
- Charcoal takes about 10 to 15 minutes to reach the proper temperature.
- When charcoal is ready for grilling, it will have an ashy coating all around, appear white or gray, and be very hot.
- For a medium fire, spread your charcoal in a single layer on the coal grate.
- For a hot fire, light enough charcoal for a double layer of coals on the coal grate.
- For an indirect fire, once the charcoal is ready, push all the charcoal to one side of the coal grate and cook on the other side of the grill.

Taking Care of the Charcoal

Unlike a gas grill, you cannot just "turn on" and "turn off" the heat with a charcoal grill. "Turning on" requires you to build a fire, and "turning off" means you have to properly shut down the grill. A good charcoal grill can be shut down when you are done by closing the lid and the vents. The lack of oxygen will stop the charcoal from burning.

That doesn't mean the charcoal is cool enough to handle; those coals will stay hot for up to 24 hours, so don't dump hot coals in the garbage or you can start a fire. Even a tiny ember can ignite a fire, so properly extinguish ashes before disposing of them.

Another option is to save the remaining charcoal. When you are done, remove the cooking grate, stir up the charcoal, replace the lid, and close the vents. Next time you grill, add fresh charcoal to what was left behind and light. If you are careful, you can cut your charcoal consumption in half and save yourself some money.

When it comes to choosing a type of charcoal, keep it clean. There are a lot of charcoals with additives. It's better to buy natural charcoal without chemicals and light naturally with a charcoal chimney, electric starter, or natural charcoal lighters. Your food will taste better and you won't fill the air with fumes.

Preparing Steaks for the Grill

Cooking steaks involve more than just taking the meat out of the fridge and slapping it on the grill. You could do that, but if you want to enjoy the perfect steak, you'll get better results if you understand a few basic guidelines for how to prep your steaks for the grill.

The first thing you're going to want to do is take the steak out of the fridge and let it sit out at room temperature for 30 minutes. At this point, you can also preheat your grill, and trim any excess fat from the steaks. But don't trim it all off. Leave about 1/4 inch of fat all the way around.

A Cold Steak Is a Tough Steak

The reason we don't want to cook chilled steaks is simple. A cold steak takes longer to cook, whether you use a pan, a grill or the broiler. The key to a perfect steak is cooking it at a high temperature for a short amount of time. The colder the steak is when it hits the grill, the longer it will take to cook it. And the more time it spends over the heat, the tougher it gets.

So just remember that a cold steak equals a tough steak. Taking the meat out of the fridge for a few minutes beforehand helps your steak stay tender and juicy.

Some people recommend leaving the meat out at room temperature for as long as an hour. The problem here is that you start to approach the territory of food safety hazard. Also, you would ideally like the interior of the meat to be a bit cool when it hits the grill. This helps you to achieve that perfect medium rare steak. If you leave the steak out for too long, the whole steak gets warm (especially if your kitchen is hot and/or it's a hot day) and you give yourself less margin for error. It's better to undercook a steak than to overcook one.

Season Steaks With Salt and Pepper

When it comes to seasoning a steak, you don't have to get too complicated about it. There are all kinds of spice rubs and seasoning mixes out there, but a perfect steak really doesn't need much more than Kosher salt and freshly ground black pepper.

Kosher salt is the best kind of salt for seasoning a steak because its coarse crystals will really grab onto the meat. Season generously. When it comes to pepper, everyone's tastes are a little different. But even a little bit of freshly ground black pepper will spice up a steak and also give it a slight crunch. But please be sure to use freshly ground black pepper and not the powdery stuff that goes in pepper shakers.

Seasoning a steak is one of those topics someone could write a whole article about, and in fact, we have. For a little more depth, check out this article on seasoning a steak.

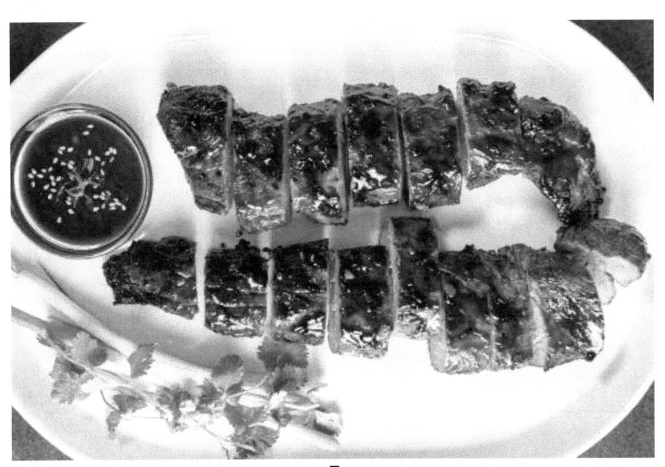

steaks from sticking to the grill and provides a bit of moisture. This is all well and good, but do you know what tastes even better than oil? Butter. So we always brush some melted butter onto my steaks before we grill them.

Clarified butter works best because it has a higher smoke point than whole butter, but if you don't have time, whole butter is fine. Alternately, use a combination of melted butter and oil. Just brush it lightly—the steak shouldn't be dripping with oil when it hits the grill, or it could start a grease fire.

How to Cook Meat and Vegetables on the Grill

A hot grill will yield a high temperature, cooking food hot and fast. For thin cuts of meat and smaller items like kebabs, steaks, chops, burgers, and hot dogs, turn up the heat and cook them quickly. The fast pace means you need to keep a close eye on the grill and more importantly, the food.

Hot and fast, however, isn't the way to grill everything. Fish, chicken, vegetables, and fruit are better grilled at lower temperatures; aim for medium heat with these foods. For a gas grill this means reducing the temperature and for charcoal, it means building a smaller fire. You still need to watch these foods closely, but they generally take longer to cook at a lower temperature.

Move Your Food Around the Grill

A common grilling myth is that you shouldn't turn grilled foods too frequently. Flip when you need to; you want even cooking. Move your foods around the grill and take advantage of the space to avoid flare-ups. However, don't be alarmed since flare-ups are bound to happen, especially with high-fat foods like steak.

8

100
BEST GRILLING
RECIPES
YOU HAVE TO TRY

Kentucky Grilled Chicken

INGREDIENTS

» 1 cup cider vinegar

» 1/2 cup canola oil

» 5 teaspoons Worcestershire sauce

» 4 teaspoons hot pepper sauce

» 2 teaspoons salt

» 10 bone-in chicken breast halves (10 ounces each)

DIRECTIONS

1. In a bowl or shallow dish, combine the first 5 ingredients. Pour 1 cup marinade into a separate bowl; add chicken and turn to coat. Cover and refrigerate for at least 4 hours. Cover and refrigerate the remaining marinade for basting.

2. Drain and discard marinade from chicken. Prepare grill for indirect heat, using a drip pan.

3. Place chicken breasts, bone side down, on oiled rack. Grill, covered, over indirect medium heat until a thermometer reads 170°, about 20 minutes on each side, basting occasionally with reserved marinade.

Gourmet Burgers with Sun-Dried Tomato

INGREDIENTS

» 1 jar (7 ounces) oil-packed sun-dried tomatoes

» 3 medium onions, halved and thinly sliced

» 3 tablespoons balsamic vinegar

» 1/2 cup finely chopped red onion

» 2 tablespoons dried basil

» 2 teaspoons ground cumin

» 2 teaspoons ground chipotle pepper

» 1/2 teaspoon salt

» 1/4 teaspoon pepper

» 3 pounds lean ground beef (90% lean)

» 1 cup crumbled goat cheese

» 8 hamburger buns, split

» Mixed salad greens, optional

DIRECTIONS

1. Drain tomatoes, reserving 1/3 cup oil; set aside. In a large skillet, saute sliced onions in 3 Tbsp. reserved oil until softened. Add vinegar. Reduce heat to medium-low; cook, stirring occasionally, until deep golden brown, 30-40 minutes.

2. Meanwhile, chop sun-dried tomatoes and transfer to a large bowl. Add the red onion, seasonings and remaining 7 tsp. of the reserved oil. Crumble beef over mixture and mix lightly but thoroughly. Shape into 16 thin patties. Place 2 tablespoons goat cheese on the center of 8 patties. Top with remaining patties and press edges firmly to seal.

3. Grill burgers, covered, over medium heat until a thermometer reads 160° and juices run clear, 5-7 minutes on each side.

4. Place buns, cut side down, on grill until toasted, 1-2 minutes. Serve burgers on buns with onions and, if desired, mixed greens.

Grilled Corn in Husks

INGREDIENTS

» 4 large ears sweet corn in husks

» 1/4 cup butter, softened

» 2 tablespoons minced fresh parsley

» 1/4 cup grated Parmesan cheese

DIRECTIONS

1. Carefully peel back husks from corn to within 1 in. of bottom; remove silk. Soak in cold water for 20 minutes; drain. Pat corn dry. Combine the butter and parsley; spread over corn. Rewrap corn in husks and secure with string.

2. Grill corn, covered, over medium heat until tender, turning often, 20-25 minutes. Serve with cheese.

Feta Salmon Salad

INGREDIENTS

» 1/4 teaspoon salt

» 1/4 teaspoon garlic powder

» 1/4 teaspoon ground ginger

» 1/4 teaspoon dried parsley flakes

» 1/4 teaspoon pepper

» 4 salmon fillets (6 ounces each)

» 1 package (5 ounces) spring mix salad greens

» 1 large cucumber, chopped

» 1 large tomato, chopped

» 1/2 cup crumbled feta cheese

» 1/4 cup red wine vinaigrette

DIRECTIONS

1. In a small bowl, mix the first 5 ingredients; sprinkle over salmon.

2. Place salmon on oiled grill rack, skin side down. Grill, covered, over medium heat or broil 4 in. from heat until fish just begins to flake easily with a fork, 10-12 minutes.

3. In a large bowl, toss salad greens with cucumber, tomato and cheese; divide among four plates. Top with salmon; drizzle with vinaigrette.

Steak Sandwiches with Crispy Onions

INGREDIENTS

» 1 large sweet onion
» 3 cups buttermilk
» 2 cups minced fresh cilantro
» 1 cup minced fresh parsley
» 2 garlic cloves, minced
» 1/2 teaspoon plus 2 teaspoons salt, divided
» 1/4 teaspoon pepper
» 1/2 cup mayonnaise
» 1/2 cup plus 3 tablespoons olive oil, divided
» 1 beef flat iron steak or top sirloin steak (1-1/2 pounds)
» 1-1/2 cups all-purpose flour
» 3 tablespoons taco seasoning
» Oil for deep-fat frying
» 12 slices Italian bread (1/2 inch thick)
» Optional: Fresh arugula and sliced tomato

DIRECTIONS

1. Cut onion into 1/4-in. slices; separate into rings. Place in a large bowl or shallow dish. Add buttermilk; turn to coat. Refrigerate at least 4 hours or overnight.

2. In a small bowl, combine cilantro, parsley, garlic, 1/2 teaspoon salt and pepper. Remove 2 tablespoons herb mixture; stir into mayonnaise. Refrigerate until serving. Stir 1/2 cup olive oil into remaining herb mixture. Reserve 2 tablespoons oil mixture for serving. Place remaining oil mixture in a large bowl or shallow dish. Add beef; turn to coat. Refrigerate at least 4 hours or overnight.

3. Drain beef, discarding marinade. Grill beef, covered, over medium heat or broil 4 in. from heat until meat reaches desired doneness, 7-9 minutes on each side (for medium-rare, a thermometer should read 135°; medium, 140°; medium-well, 145°).

4. Meanwhile, drain onion rings, discarding marinade. In a shallow dish, combine flour, taco seasoning and remaining 2 teaspoons salt. Roll onion rings in flour mixture. In an electric skillet or deep-fat fryer, heat 1 in. of oil to 375°. Fry onion rings, a few at a time, until golden brown, 1 to 1-1/2 minutes on each side. Drain on paper towels; keep warm.

5. Remove steak to a cutting board; brush with reserved 2 tablespoons oil mixture. Brush bread with remaining 3 tablespoons olive oil. Grill bread over medium heat until toasted, 30-60 seconds on each side.

6. Spread mayonnaise mixture over 1 side of each toast. Thinly slice steak. Top 6 slices of toast with steak, fried onions and, if desired, arugula and tomato slices. Top with remaining toast.

Grilled Caesar Chicken Breasts

INGREDIENTS

» 1/2 cup creamy Caesar salad dressing

» 3 tablespoons olive oil

» 3 tablespoons Dijon mustard

» 6 garlic cloves, minced

» 4 boneless skinless chicken breast halves (6 ounces each)

DIRECTIONS

1. In a shallow dish, combine dressing, oil, mustard and garlic. Add chicken; turn to coat. Cover and refrigerate for 8 hours or overnight.

2. Drain and discard marinade. Grill chicken, covered, over medium heat or broil 4 in. from the heat until a thermometer reads 165°, 7-8 minutes on each side.

The Best Grilled Sirloin Tip Roast

INGREDIENTS

» 1 beef sirloin tip roast or beef tri-tip roast (2 to 3 pounds)

» 1 tablespoon kosher salt

» 2 teaspoons dried thyme

» 2 teaspoons garlic powder

» 1 teaspoon coarsely ground pepper

» 1 small onion, chopped

» 2 tablespoons olive oil, divided

» 1 bottle (750 milliliters) dry red wine

» 6 fresh thyme sprigs

» 1 garlic cloves, crushed

» 1/2 teaspoon whole peppercorns

» 3 whole cloves

» HORSERADISH-THYME BUTTER (OPTIONAL):

» 6 tablespoons softened butter

» 2 tablespoons prepared horseradish

» 3 tablespoons fresh thyme leaves

DIRECTIONS

1. Sprinkle roast with salt, thyme, garlic powder and ground pepper. Cover and refrigerate at least 8 hours or up to 24 hours. Meanwhile, in a saucepan, saute onion in 1 tablespoon oil until tender, about 5 minutes. Add wine, thyme, garlic, peppercorns and cloves. Simmer until reduced to 3/4 cup. Cool; strain, discarding solids, and refrigerate.

2. Remove roast from the refrigerator 1 hour before grilling. Prepare grill for indirect heat, using a drip pan. Add wood chips according to manufacturer's directions.

3. Pat roast dry with paper towels. Brush with remaining 1 tablespoon oil; place over drip pan. Grill, covered, over medium-low indirect heat, brushing with mop sauce every 20 minutes, until meat reaches desired doneness (for medium-rare, a thermometer should read 135°; medium, 140°; medium-well, 145°), 1-1/2 to 2 hours. Let stand 15 minutes before slicing.

4. If desired, in a small bowl, stir together butter, horseradish and thyme. Serve on top of roast.

Fresh Corn & Arugula Salad

INGREDIENTS

BASIL VINAIGRETTE:

» 1/2 cup olive oil

» 1/4 cup balsamic vinegar

» 3 tablespoons minced fresh basil

» 1 teaspoon chopped shallot

» 1 teaspoon minced fresh rosemary

» 1 teaspoon lemon juice

» 1/4 teaspoon salt

» 1/4 teaspoon pepper

SALAD:

» 2 ears fresh corn, husked

» 1 teaspoon olive oil

» 8 cups fresh arugula or baby spinach

» 4 plum tomatoes, quartered

» 1/4 cup pecan halves, toasted

» 1/4 cup shaved Parmesan cheese

DIRECTIONS

1. In a small bowl, whisk vinaigrette ingredients until blended.

2. Brush corn with oil; grill, covered, over medium heat or broil 4 in. from heat 8-10 minutes or until corn is crisp-tender and browned, turning occasionally. When cool enough to handle, cut corn off cobs and place in a large bowl.

3. Add arugula, tomatoes and pecans to corn. Drizzle with half of the vinaigrette; toss to coat. Top with cheese; serve immediately. Cover and refrigerate remaining vinaigrette for later use.

INGREDIENTS

» 4 salmon fillets (4 ounces each)

» 1 teaspoon garlic powder

» 1 teaspoon lemon-pepper seasoning

» 1 teaspoon curry powder

» 1/2 teaspoon salt

» 1 small onion, cut into rings

» 2 medium tomatoes, seeded and chopped

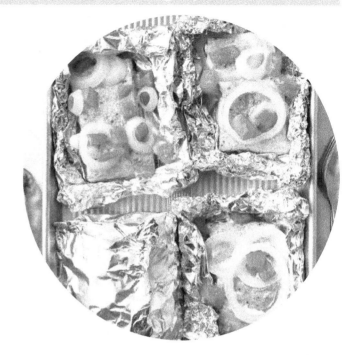

DIRECTIONS

1. Place salmon, skin side down, on a double thickness of heavy-duty foil (about 18x12 in.). Combine the garlic powder, lemon pepper, curry and salt; sprinkle over salmon. Top with onion and tomatoes. Fold foil over fish and seal tightly.

2. Grill, covered, over medium heat for 10-15 minutes or until fish flakes easily with a fork. Open foil carefully to allow steam to escape.

Grilled Elote Flatbread

INGREDIENTS

» 2 medium ears sweet corn, husked

» 3 tablespoons olive oil, divided

» 1 pound fresh or frozen pizza dough, thawed

» 1/2 cup mayonnaise

» 1/3 cup crumbled Cotija cheese, divided

» 1/3 cup chopped fresh cilantro, divided

» 1 tablespoon lime juice

» 1/2 teaspoon chili powder

» 1/8 teaspoon pepper

DIRECTIONS

1. Brush corn with 1 tablespoon oil. Grill corn, covered, over medium heat until lightly browned and tender, 10-12 minutes, turning occasionally. Cool slightly. Cut corn from cobs; transfer to a large bowl.

2. On a lightly floured surface, roll or press dough into a 15x10-in. oval (about 1/4 in. thick); place on a greased sheet of foil. Brush top with 1 tablespoon oil.

3. Carefully invert crust onto grill rack, removing foil. Brush top with remaining 1 tablespoon oil. Grill, covered, over medium heat until bottom is golden brown, 2-3 minutes on each side. Remove from grill; cool slightly.

4. Add mayonnaise, 3 tablespoons cheese, 3 tablespoons cilantro, lime juice, chili powder and pepper to corn; stir to combine. Spread over warm crust. Sprinkle with remaining cheese and cilantro.

Grilled Romaine Salad

INGREDIENTS

» 1/3 cup plus 3 tablespoons olive oil, divided

» 2 tablespoons white wine vinegar

» 1 tablespoon dill weed

» 1/2 teaspoon garlic powder

» 1/8 teaspoon crushed red pepper flakes

» 1/8 teaspoon salt

» 6 green onions

» 4 plum tomatoes, halved

» 1 large cucumber, peeled and halved lengthwise

» 2 romaine hearts

DIRECTIONS

1. In a small bowl, whisk 1/3 cup oil, vinegar and seasonings. Set aside.

2. Brush the onions, tomatoes, cucumber and romaine with remaining oil. Grill the onions, tomatoes and cucumber, uncovered, over medium heat for 4-5 minutes on each side or until onions are crisp-tender. Grill romaine for 30 seconds on each side or until heated through.

3. Chop the vegetables; place in a large bowl. Whisk dressing and pour over salad; toss to coat. Serve immediately.

Grilled Onion & Skirt Steak Tacos

INGREDIENTS

» 2 beef skirt or flank steaks (1 pound each)

» 1 bottle (12 ounces) beer

» 1/4 cup lime juice

» 3 tablespoons olive oil, divided

» 8 spring onions or green onions

» 1-1/4 teaspoons salt, divided

» 3/4 teaspoon pepper, divided

» Corn tortillas, minced fresh cilantro and lime wedges

DIRECTIONS

1. Pound beef with a meat mallet to tenderize. In a large bowl, mix beer, lime juice and 2 tablespoons oil until blended. Add beef to marinade; turn to coat. Refrigerate, covered, at least 30 minutes.

2. Meanwhile, cut partially through onions, leaving tops intact. Drizzle with remaining oil; sprinkle with 1/4 teaspoon salt and 1/4 teaspoon pepper.

3. Drain beef, discarding marinade; sprinkle with the remaining salt and pepper. On a greased grill rack, grill steaks and onions, covered, over medium heat or broil 4 in. from heat until meat reaches desired doneness (for medium-rare, a thermometer should read 135°; medium, 140°; medium-well, 145°) and onions are crisp-tender, 2-4 minutes on each side. Cut steak diagonally across the grain into thin slices. Serve with tortillas, onions, cilantro and lime wedges.

Margarita Chicken

INGREDIENTS

» 1 can (12 ounces) frozen nonalcoholic margarita mix, thawed

» 3 tablespoons lime juice

» 3 garlic cloves, minced

» 4 boneless skinless chicken breast halves (6 ounces each)

» 1/4 teaspoon salt

» 1/4 teaspoon pepper

DIRECTIONS

1. In a small bowl, combine margarita mix, lime juice and garlic. Pour 1 cup marinade into a shallow dish. Add chicken; turn to coat. Cover and refrigerate for 2-4 hours. Cover and refrigerate remaining marinade.

2. Drain chicken, discarding marinade. Sprinkle chicken with salt and pepper. Place chicken on oiled grill rack. Grill, covered, over medium heat (or broil 4 in. from heat) until a thermometer reads 165°, 5-7 minutes on each side, basting frequently with reserved marinade.

Grilled Flank Steak

INGREDIENTS

» 1/4 cup soy sauce

» 2 tablespoons white vinegar

» 1 green onion, sliced

» 1-1/2 teaspoons garlic powder

» 1-1/2 teaspoons ground ginger

» 3 tablespoons honey

» 3/4 cup vegetable oil

» 1 beef flank steak (about 1-1/2 pounds)

» 1 pound fresh mushrooms, sliced

» 1 green pepper, cut into thin strips

» 1 yellow or sweet red pepper, cut into thin strips

» 3 carrots, cut into julienned strips

DIRECTIONS

1. In a bowl, combine the first seven ingredients. Pour 3/4 cup marinade into a shallow dish; add the beef. Turn to coat; refrigerate, covered, for up to 24 hours, turning once. Cover and refrigerate remaining marinade.

2. Drain and discard marinade. Grill flank steak, uncovered, over medium heat for 6-8 minutes on each side or until meat reaches desired doneness (for medium-rare, a thermometer should read 135°; medium, 140°; medium-well, 145°).

3. Meanwhile, in a skillet, cook vegetables in reserved marinade until crisp-tender. Thinly slice steak across the grain. Serve with vegetables.

Dry-Rub Grilled Pork Chops over Cannellini Greens

INGREDIENTS

» 1 tablespoon olive oil

» 1 medium onion, chopped

» 2 garlic cloves, minced

» 1 can (15 ounces) cannellini beans, rinsed and drained

» 1 cup water-packed artichoke hearts, drained and chopped

» 3/4 cup pitted Greek olives, chopped

» 1/4 cup dry white wine or chicken broth

» 1/4 cup chicken broth

» 1/4 teaspoon salt

» 1/4 teaspoon smoked paprika

» 1/4 teaspoon pepper

» 4 bone-in pork loin chops (8 ounces each)

» 2 teaspoons Greek seasoning or seasoning of your choice

» 5 ounces fresh baby spinach (about 6 cups)

DIRECTIONS

1. In a large skillet, heat oil over medium-high heat. Add onion; cook and stir until tender 4-5 minutes. Add garlic; cook 1 minute longer. Stir in beans, artichokes, olives, wine, broth, salt. paprika and pepper. Bring to a boil; reduce heat. Simmer until liquid is almost evaporated, 12-15 minutes.

2. Meanwhile, sprinkle chops with Greek seasoning. Grill pork chops over medium heat until a thermometer reads 145°, 6-8 minutes on each side. Let stand 5 minutes before serving.

3. Stir spinach into bean mixture; cook and stir until wilted, 2-3 minutes. Serve with pork.

Grilled Chicken Salad

INGREDIENTS

» 1 package (16 ounces) elbow macaroni, ziti or spiral pasta

» 6 boneless skinless chicken breast halves (6 ounces each)

» 2 tablespoons lemon juice

» 2-1/2 cups sliced celery

» 1 medium red onion, chopped

» 1 medium sweet red pepper, chopped

» 1/4 cup minced fresh dill or 5 teaspoons dill weed

» 3 tablespoons white wine vinegar

» 2 tablespoons mayonnaise

» 2 tablespoons Dijon mustard

» 1/2 teaspoon salt

» 1/4 teaspoon pepper

» 2/3 cup olive oil

» Leaf lettuce

» Snipped fresh dill, optional

DIRECTIONS

1. Cook pasta according to package directions. Grill chicken, uncovered, over medium heat until juices run clear, 5-8 minutes on each side. Remove from grill to a rimmed platter. Sprinkle with lemon juice; let stand 10 minutes. Drain pasta; rinse with cold water.

2. Remove chicken from platter to a cutting board and cut into strips; pour juices into a large bowl. To the juices, add vinegar, mayonnaise, mustard, salt and pepper; whisk well. Gradually whisk in oil. Add pasta, celery, onion, red pepper and dill; toss to coat. Arrange pasta over lettuce-lined plates. Top with chicken. If desired, sprinkle with dill.

Halibut Soft Tacos

Total Time: Prep/Total Time: 30 min.   Servings: 4

INGREDIENTS

» 1 medium mango, peeled and cubed

» 1/2 cup cubed avocado

» 1/4 cup chopped red onion

» 2 tablespoons chopped seeded jalapeno pepper

» 1 tablespoon minced fresh cilantro

» 3 teaspoons olive oil, divided

» 1 teaspoon lemon juice

» 1 teaspoon honey

» 1 pound halibut steaks (3/4 inch thick)

» 1/2 teaspoon salt

» 1/4 teaspoon pepper

» 4 Bibb lettuce leaves

» 4 flour tortillas (6 inches), warmed

» 4 teaspoons sweet Thai chili sauce

DIRECTIONS

1. In a small bowl, combine the mango, avocado, onion, jalapeno, cilantro, 2 teaspoons oil, lemon juice and honey; set aside. Brush halibut with remaining oil; sprinkle with salt and pepper.

2. Grill halibut on greased rack, covered, over high heat or broil 3-4 in. from the heat until fish flakes easily with a fork, 3-5 minutes on each side.

3. Place lettuce leaves on tortillas; top with fish and mango mixture. Drizzle with chili sauce.

Brined Grilled Turkey Breast

INGREDIENTS

» 2 quarts cold water, divided

» 1/2 cup kosher salt

» 1/2 cup packed brown sugar

» 1 tablespoon whole peppercorns

» 1 boneless skinless turkey breast half (2 to 3 pounds)

» BASTING SAUCE:

» 1/4 cup canola oil

» 1/4 cup sesame oil

» 1/4 cup reduced-sodium soy sauce

» 3 tablespoons lemon juice

» 2 tablespoons honey

» 3 garlic cloves, minced

» 1/4 teaspoon dried thyme

» 1/4 teaspoon crushed red pepper flakes

DIRECTIONS

1. In a large saucepan, combine 1 quart water, salt, brown sugar and peppercorns. Bring to a boil. Cook and stir until salt and sugar are dissolved. Pour into a large bowl. Add remaining 1 quart cold water to cool the brine to room temperature. Add turkey breast; turn to coat. Cover and refrigerate 4-6 hours, turning occasionally.

2. Prepare grill for indirect medium heat, using a drip pan. Meanwhile, combine basting sauce ingredients. Grill turkey, covered, until a thermometer reads 170°, 1-1/4 to 1-1/2 hours, basting occasionally with sauce. Remove to a cutting board. Cover and let stand 10 minutes before slicing.

Grilled Mahi Mahi

INGREDIENTS

» 3/4 cup reduced-sodium teriyaki sauce

» 2 tablespoons sherry or pineapple juice

» 2 garlic cloves

» 8 mahi mahi fillets (6 ounces each)

TROPICAL FRUIT SALSA:

» 1 medium mango, peeled and diced

» 1 cup chopped seeded peeled papaya

» 3/4 cup chopped green pepper

» 1/2 cup cubed fresh pineapple

» 1/2 medium red onion, chopped

» 1/4 cup minced fresh cilantro

» 1/4 cup minced fresh mint

» 1 tablespoon chopped seeded jalapeno pepper

» 1 tablespoon lime juice

» 1 tablespoon lemon juice

» 1/2 teaspoon crushed red pepper flakes

DIRECTIONS

1. In a shallow dish, combine the teriyaki sauce, sherry or pineapple juice and garlic; add mahi mahi. Turn to coat; refrigerate for 30 minutes.

2. Meanwhile, in a large bowl, combine the salsa ingredients. Cover and refrigerate until serving.

3. Drain and discard marinade. Place mahi mahi on an oiled grill rack. Grill, covered, over medium heat or broil 4 in. from the heat for 4-5 minutes on each side or until fish flakes easily with a fork. Serve with salsa.

Beef 'n' Pork Burgers

INGREDIENTS

» 4 bacon strips, diced

» 1 large onion, finely chopped

» 1 garlic clove, minced

» 1-1/2 cups soft bread crumbs

» 1 large egg, lightly beaten

» 1/2 cup water

» 1 tablespoon dried parsley flakes

» 2 to 3 teaspoons salt

» 1/4 teaspoon dried marjoram

» 1/4 teaspoon paprika

» 1/4 teaspoon pepper

» 1 pound ground beef

» 1 pound ground pork

» 8 hamburger buns, split and toasted

» Mayonnaise, lettuce leaves, red onion, and tomato slices

DIRECTIONS

1. In a small skillet, cook bacon, onion and garlic over medium heat until the bacon is crisp; drain and place in a small bowl. Stir in the bread crumbs, egg, water, parsley, salt, marjoram, paprika and pepper. Crumble beef and pork over the mixture and mix well. Shape into eight 3/4-in.-thick patties.

2. Grill, uncovered, over medium-hot heat for 4-5 minutes on each side or until a thermometer reads 160°. Serve on buns with mayonnaise, lettuce and tomato.

The Best Baby Back Ribs

INGREDIENTS

» 2 racks baby back ribs (about 4-1/2 pounds)

» 3/4 cup chicken broth

» 3/4 cup soy sauce

» 1 cup sugar, divided

» 6 tablespoons cider vinegar

» 6 tablespoons olive oil

» 3 garlic cloves, minced

» 2 teaspoons salt

» 1 tablespoon paprika

» 1/2 teaspoon chili powder

» 1/2 teaspoon pepper

» 1/4 teaspoon garlic powder

» Dash cayenne pepper

» Barbecue sauce, optional

DIRECTIONS

1. If necessary, remove thin membrane from ribs and discard. Combine broth, soy sauce, 1/2 cup sugar, vinegar, olive oil and garlic. Place ribs in a shallow baking dish; pour two-thirds of the marinade over ribs. Turn to coat; refrigerate overnight, turning occasionally. Cover and refrigerate remaining marinade.

2. Drain ribs, discarding marinade. Combine remaining sugar, salt and seasonings; rub over both sides of ribs.

3. Grill ribs, covered, on an oiled rack over indirect medium heat for 30 minutes on each side.

4. Baste with reserved marinade, or, if desired, barbecue sauce. Move ribs to direct medium heat and cook until pork is tender, turning and basting occasionally, 20-40 minutes longer.

Chicken Strawberry Spinach Salad

INGREDIENTS

» 3/4 pound boneless skinless chicken breasts, cut into strips

» 1/4 cup reduced-sodium chicken broth

» 1/4 cup poppy seed salad dressing, divided

» 2 cups fresh baby spinach

» 1 cup torn romaine

» 1 cup sliced fresh strawberries

» 1/4 cup sliced almonds, toasted

DIRECTIONS

1. Place chicken on a double thickness of heavy-duty foil (about 18 in. x 15 in.). Combine broth and 1 tablespoon poppy seed dressing; spoon over chicken. Fold edges of foil around chicken mixture, leaving center open. Grill, covered, over medium heat until chicken is no longer pink, 10-12 minutes.

2. In a large salad bowl, combine the spinach, romaine and strawberries. Add chicken and the remaining poppy seed dressing; toss to coat. Sprinkle with almonds.

Grilled Asparagus

INGREDIENTS

» 1 cup water

» 1 pound fresh asparagus, trimmed

» 1/4 cup barbecue sauce

DIRECTIONS

1. In a large skillet, bring water to a boil; add asparagus. Cover and cook until crisp-tender, about 2-3 minutes; drain and pat dry. Cool Slightly.

2. Thread several asparagus spears onto 2 parallel soaked wooden skewers. Repeat. Grill, uncovered, over medium heat for 2 minutes, turning once. Baste with barbecue sauce. Grill 2 minutes longer, turning and basting once.

INGREDIENTS

» 1 medium sweet red pepper, chopped

» 1 medium onion, chopped

» 2 tablespoons olive oil

» 4 cups instant brown rice

» 4 garlic cloves, minced

» 1 chipotle pepper in adobo sauce, chopped

» 6 cups reduced-sodium chicken broth

» 1 can (14-1/2 ounces) no-salt-added diced tomatoes

» 1 teaspoon saffron threads or 4 teaspoons ground turmeric

» 1 pound uncooked medium shrimp, peeled and deveined

» 1 package (12 ounces) fully cooked chorizo chicken sausage or flavor of your choice, cut into 1/4-inch slices

» 1 medium mango, coarsely chopped

» 2 tablespoons lime juice

» 1/4 teaspoon cayenne pepper

» 1 medium lime, cut into wedges

» 2 tablespoons minced fresh cilantro

DIRECTIONS

1. In a Dutch oven, saute red pepper and onion in oil until tender. Add the rice, garlic and chipotle pepper; saute 2 minutes longer. Add the broth, tomatoes and saffron. Bring to a boil. Reduce heat; cover and simmer until liquid is absorbed, about 5 minutes. Let stand for 5 minutes.

2. Meanwhile, in a large bowl, combine the shrimp, chicken sausage and mango; sprinkle with lime juice and cayenne. Transfer to a grill wok or basket. Grill, covered, over medium heat until shrimp turn pink, 5-8 minutes, stirring occasionally.

3. Add shrimp mixture to Dutch oven; toss to combine. Garnish with lime wedges and cilantro.

Artichoke Steak Wraps

INGREDIENTS

» 8 ounces frozen artichoke hearts (about 2 cups), thawed and chopped

» 2 medium tomatoes, chopped

» 1/4 cup chopped fresh cilantro

» 3/4 teaspoon salt, divided

» 1 pound beef flat iron or top sirloin steak (1-1/4 pounds)

» 1/4 teaspoon pepper

6 whole wheat tortillas (8 inches), warmed

DIRECTIONS

1. Toss artichoke hearts and tomatoes with cilantro and 1/4 teaspoon salt.

2. Sprinkle steak with pepper and remaining salt. Grill, covered, over medium heat or broil 4 in. from heat until meat reaches desired doneness (for medium-rare, a thermometer should read 135°; medium, 140°), 5-6 minutes per side. Remove from heat; let stand 5 minutes. Cut into thin slices. Serve steak and salsa in tortillas, folding bottoms and sides of tortillas to close.

Lemon-Dijon Grilled Salmon Foil Packet

INGREDIENTS

- » 4 salmon fillets (4 ounces each)
- » 4 teaspoons olive oil
- » 4 teaspoons lemon juice
- » 1 tablespoon drained capers
- » 1 tablespoon Dijon mustard
- » 2 garlic cloves, minced
- » 1/2 teaspoon dill weed
- » 1/2 teaspoon dried thyme
- » 1/4 teaspoon salt
- » 1/8 teaspoon cayenne pepper

DIRECTIONS

1. Place each salmon fillet on a double thickness of heavy-duty foil (about 12 in. square). Combine the remaining ingredients; spoon over salmon. Fold foil around fish and seal tightly.

2. Grill, covered, over medium heat for 10-15 minutes or until fish flakes easily with a fork. Open foil carefully to allow steam to escape.

Easy Grilled Corn with Chipotle-Lime Butter

INGREDIENTS

» 8 large ears sweet corn in husks

» 1/2 cup butter, softened

» 1-1/2 teaspoons grated lime zest

» 1 teaspoon minced fresh cilantro

» 1/2 teaspoon salt

» 1/2 teaspoon ground chipotle pepper

» Coarse sea salt, optional

DIRECTIONS

1. In a large stockpot, cover corn with cold water. Soak 30 minutes; drain. Grill corn, covered, over medium heat until tender, turning occasionally, 25-30 minutes.

2. Meanwhile, combine next 5 ingredients. Carefully peel back husks; discard silk. Spread butter mixture over corn. If desired, sprinkle with coarse sea salt.

Grilled Steak Tacos

INGREDIENTS

SPICY AIOLI:

» 1/4 cup mayonnaise

» 2 teaspoons Sriracha chili sauce or 1 teaspoon hot pepper sauce

» 1/8 teaspoon sesame oil

AVOCADO-CORN SALSA:

» 1 medium ripe avocado, peeled and finely chopped

» 1/2 medium tomato, seeded and chopped

» 3 tablespoons sliced ripe olives

» 2 tablespoons canned whole kernel corn

» 2 tablespoons chopped sweet red pepper

» 2 tablespoons lime juice

» 4 teaspoons minced fresh cilantro

» 1 teaspoon kosher salt

» 1 teaspoon finely chopped onion

» 1 garlic clove, minced

» 1/4 teaspoon ground cumin

STEAKS:

» 2 teaspoons pepper

» 2 teaspoons olive oil

» 1 teaspoon kosher salt

» 1 teaspoon seafood seasoning

» 1 beef ribeye steak (1 pound), trimmed

» 8 flour tortillas (6 inches)

» Optional toppings: Shredded lettuce, cheddar cheese and Cotija cheese

DIRECTIONS

1. In a small bowl, combine the aioli ingredients. In another bowl, combine the salsa ingredients. Refrigerate until serving.

2. Combine the pepper, oil, salt and seafood seasoning; rub over both sides of steak.

3. Grill, covered, over medium heat until meat reaches desired doneness (for medium-rare, a thermometer should read 135°; medium, 140°; medium-well, 145°), 6-8 minutes on each side. Let stand for 5 minutes.

4. Meanwhile, grill tortillas until warm, about 45 seconds on each side. Thinly slice steak; place on tortillas. Serve with aioli, salsa and toppings of your choice.

Grilled Fruit Phyllo Tart

INGREDIENTS

» 3 tablespoons butter, melted

» 4 teaspoons canola oil

» 8 sheets phyllo dough (14x9-inch size)

» 1 large lemon

» 3 medium peaches, peeled and halved

» 2 cups large fresh strawberries, stems removed

» 4 slices fresh pineapple (1/2 inch thick)

» 1/3 cup packed brown sugar

» 1/2 teaspoon salt

» 1/2 cup heavy whipping cream

» 1 package (8 ounces) cream cheese, softened

» 1/3 cup confectioners' sugar

» 2 tablespoons chopped fresh mint

DIRECTIONS

1. Preheat oven to 400°. In a small bowl, mix butter and oil. Brush a 15x10x1-in. baking pan with some of the butter mixture. Place 1 sheet of phyllo dough into prepared pan; brush with butter mixture. Layer with 7 additional phyllo sheets, brushing each layer. (Keep remaining phyllo covered with a damp towel to prevent it from drying out.) Bake 5-7 minutes or until golden brown (phyllo will puff up during baking). Cool completely.

2. Finely grate 1 Tbsp. lemon zest. Cut lemon crosswise in half; squeeze juice into a bowl. In a large bowl, toss peaches, strawberries, pineapple, brown sugar, salt, and lemon zest and juice. Remove strawberries; thread fruit onto 3 metal or soaked wooden skewers.

3. Place fruit on oiled grill rack. Grill, covered, over medium heat until fruit is tender, turning once, 8-10 minutes for pineapple slices and peaches, 4-5 minutes for strawberries. Remove and set aside.

4. In a small bowl, beat cream until soft peaks form. In another bowl, beat cream cheese and confectioners' sugar until smooth. Fold in whipped cream. Spread over phyllo crust. Slice grilled fruit; arrange over filling. Sprinkle with mint; cut into pieces.

California Burger Wraps

INGREDIENTS

» 1 pound lean ground beef (90% lean)

» 1/2 teaspoon salt

» 1/4 teaspoon pepper

» 8 Bibb lettuce leaves

» 1/3 cup crumbled feta cheese

» 2 tablespoons Miracle Whip Light

» 1/2 medium ripe avocado, peeled and cut into 8 slices

» 1/4 cup chopped red onion

» Chopped cherry tomatoes, optional

DIRECTIONS

1. In a large bowl, combine beef, salt and pepper, mixing lightly but thoroughly. Shape into eight 1/2-in.-thick patties.

2. Grill burgers, covered, over medium heat or broil 3-4 in. from heat until a thermometer reads 160°, 3-4 minutes on each side. Place burgers in lettuce leaves. Combine feta and Miracle Whip; spread over burgers. Top with avocado, red onion and, if desired, tomatoes.

Bratwurst and Chicken Kabobs

INGREDIENTS

» 1/4 cup balsamic vinegar

» 1/4 cup cider vinegar

» 2 tablespoons pepper jelly

» 2 tablespoons stone-ground mustard

» 1 teaspoon salt

» 1/2 teaspoon pepper

» 1/2 cup olive oil, divided

» 1 can (15 ounces) peach halves in light syrup, drained and cut into 1/2-in. cubes

» 2/3 cup minced onion

» 1 jar (12 ounces) mango chutney

» 6 boneless skinless chicken breasts (6 ounces each)

» 1 package (14 ounces) fully cooked bratwurst links

» 2 each medium green pepper, sweet red pepper and yellow pepper

» 1 large onion

» 3 tablespoons brown sugar bourbon seasoning

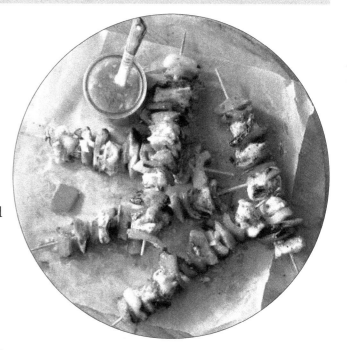

DIRECTIONS

1. Whisk together vinegars, pepper jelly, mustard, salt and pepper. Gradually whisk in 1/3 cup olive oil until blended. Add peaches, minced onion and chutney.

2. Cut chicken into 1-in. cubes and bratwursts into 1-in. slices. Cut peppers into large squares and onion into cubes. Toss with brown sugar bourbon seasoning and remaining oil.

3. On 12 metal or soaked wooden skewers, alternately thread meat and vegetables. Grill skewers, covered, on a greased grill rack over medium-high direct heat, turning occasionally, until chicken is no longer pink and vegetables are tender, 10-12 minutes. If desired, sprinkle with additional brown sugar bourbon seasoning during grilling. Serve with chutney.

Aloha Burgers

INGREDIENTS

- » 1 can (8 ounces) sliced pineapple
- » 3/4 cup reduced-sodium teriyaki sauce
- » 1 pound ground beef
- » 1 large sweet onion, sliced
- » 1 tablespoon butter
- » 4 lettuce leaves
- » 4 sesame seed or onion buns, split and toasted
- » 4 slices Swiss cheese
- » 4 bacon strips, cooked

DIRECTIONS

1. Drain pineapple juice into a small bowl; add teriyaki sauce. Place 3 tablespoons in a resealable plastic bag. Add pineapple slices; toss to coat and set aside.

2. Shape beef into four patties; place in an 8-in. square baking dish. Pour the remaining teriyaki sauce mixture over patties; marinate for 5-10 minutes, turning once.

3. Remove burger patties from marinade; discard marinade. Grill, covered, over medium heat or broil 4 in. from the heat for 6-9 minutes on each side or until a thermometer reads 160°. Meanwhile, in a small skillet, saute onion in butter until tender, about 5 minutes; set aside.

4. Remove pineapple slices from marinade; discard marinade. Place pineapple on grill or under broiler to heat through. Layer bottom buns with lettuce and onion. Top with burgers, cheese, pineapple and bacon. Replace tops.

Grilled Bruschetta

INGREDIENTS

- » 1/2 cup balsamic vinegar
- » 1-1/2 cups chopped and seeded plum tomatoes
- » 2 tablespoons finely chopped shallot
- » 1 tablespoon minced fresh basil
- » 2 teaspoons plus 3 tablespoons olive oil, divided
- » 1 garlic clove, minced
- » 16 slices French bread baguette (1/2 inch thick)
- » Sea salt and grated Parmesan cheese

DIRECTIONS

1. In a small saucepan, bring vinegar to a boil; cook until liquid is reduced to 3 tablespoons, 8-10 minutes. Remove from heat. Meanwhile, combine tomatoes, shallot, basil, 2 teaspoons olive oil and garlic. Cover and refrigerate until serving.

2. Brush remaining oil over both sides of baguette slices. Grill, uncovered, over medium heat until golden brown on both sides.

3. Top toasts with tomato mixture. Drizzle with balsamic syrup; sprinkle with sea salt and Parmesan. Serve immediately.

INGREDIENTS

» 2 large ears sweet corn, husked

» 1 teaspoon butter, softened

» 1/8 teaspoon salt

» 1/8 teaspoon pepper

» 1 haddock fillet (8 ounces)

» 2 teaspoons chili powder, divided

» 2 cups shredded lettuce

» 2 medium tomatoes, seeded and chopped

» 1 medium sweet red pepper, chopped

» 1 medium ripe avocado, peeled and chopped

» 3 tablespoons taco sauce

» 2 tablespoons lime juice, divided

» 1 tablespoon minced fresh cilantro

» 1-1/2 teaspoons grated lime zest

» 12 flour tortillas (8 inches)

DIRECTIONS

1. Spread corn with butter and sprinkle with salt and pepper. Grill, covered, over medium heat until tender, 10-12 minutes, turning occasionally.

2. Meanwhile, sprinkle fish with 1 teaspoon chili powder. On a lightly oiled grill rack, grill fish, covered, over medium heat until fish flakes easily with a fork, 7-9 minutes.

3. Cool corn slightly; remove kernels from cobs. Place in a large bowl. Add the lettuce, tomatoes, red pepper, avocado, taco sauce, 1 tablespoon lime juice, cilantro, lime zest and the remaining chili powder.

4. Drizzle remaining lime juice over fish; cut into 1/2-in. cubes.

5. Add fish to corn mixture. Spoon 1/2 cup mixture over each tortilla. Serve immediately.

Big John's Chili-Rubbed Ribs

INGREDIENTS

» 3 tablespoons packed brown sugar

» 2 tablespoons paprika

» 2 tablespoons chili powder

» 3 teaspoons ground cumin

» 2 teaspoons garlic powder

» 1 teaspoon salt

» 6 pounds pork baby back ribs

» GLAZE:

» 1 cup reduced-sodium soy sauce

» 1 cup packed brown sugar

» 2/3 cup ketchup

» 1/3 cup lemon juice

» 1-1/2 teaspoons minced fresh gingerroot

DIRECTIONS

1. Mix the first 6 ingredients; rub over ribs. Refrigerate, covered, 30 minutes.

2. Wrap rib racks in large pieces of heavy-duty foil; seal tightly. Grill, covered, over indirect medium heat until tender, 1 to 1-1/2 hours.

3. In a large saucepan, combine glaze ingredients; cook, uncovered, over medium heat until heated through and sugar is dissolved, 6-8 minutes, stirring occasionally.

4. Carefully remove ribs from foil. Place ribs over direct heat; brush with some of the glaze. Grill, covered, over medium heat until browned, 25-30 minutes, turning and brushing ribs occasionally with remaining glaze.

Cajun Grilled Shrimp

INGREDIENTS

» 3 green onions, finely chopped

» 2 tablespoons lemon juice

» 1 tablespoon olive oil

» 3 garlic cloves, minced

» 2 teaspoons paprika

» 1 teaspoon salt

» 1/4 teaspoon pepper

» 1/4 teaspoon cayenne pepper

» 2 pounds uncooked medium shrimp, peeled and deveined with tails on

» 4 medium lemons, each cut into 8 wedges

DIRECTIONS

1. In a large shallow dish, combine the first 8 ingredients. Add shrimp and turn to coat. Cover; refrigerate for 15 minutes.

2. Drain shrimp, discarding marinade. On 12 metal or soaked wooden skewers, thread shrimp and lemon wedges.

3. Grill, covered, over medium heat or broil 4 in. from the heat until shrimp turn pink, turning once, 6-8 minutes.

Grilled Pork and Poblano Peppers

Total Time: Prep: 10 min. Grill 20 min.   Servings: 6

INGREDIENTS

» 3 large poblano peppers

» 1-1/2 cups shredded Monterey Jack cheese

» 4-1/2 teaspoons chili powder

» 1-1/2 teaspoons onion powder

» 1-1/2 teaspoons ground cumin

» 1/2 teaspoon garlic powder

» 1/4 teaspoon salt

» 1/8 teaspoon aniseed, ground

» 1/8 teaspoon cayenne pepper

» 2 pork tenderloins (about 1 pound each)

DIRECTIONS

1. Cut each pepper in half and remove the seeds. Stuff peppers with cheese; set aside.

2. Combine the seasonings; rub over pork. Grill, covered, over medium-hot heat until a thermometer reads 145°, about 15 minutes. Place peppers over indirect heat; cook until peppers are tender and cheese is melted, about 8-10 minutes.

Grilled Lobster Tails

INGREDIENTS

» 6 frozen lobster tails (8 to 10 ounces each), thawed

» 3/4 cup olive oil

» 3 tablespoons minced fresh chives

» 3 garlic cloves, minced

» 1/2 teaspoon salt

» 1/2 teaspoon pepper

DIRECTIONS

1. Using scissors, cut 3 to 4 lengthwise slits in underside of tail to loosen shell slightly. Cut top of lobster shell lengthwise down the center with scissors, leaving tail fin intact. Cut shell at an angle away from the center of the tail at base of tail fin. Loosen meat from shell, keeping the fin end attached; lift meat and lay over shell.

2. In a small bowl, combine the remaining ingredients; spoon over lobster meat. Cover and refrigerate for 20 minutes.

3. Place lobster tails, meat side up, on grill rack. Grill, covered, over medium heat for 10-12 minutes or until meat is opaque.

Grilled Stone Fruits with Balsamic Syrup

INGREDIENTS

» 1/2 cup balsamic vinegar

» 2 tablespoons brown sugar

» 2 medium peaches, peeled and halved

» 2 medium nectarines, peeled and halved

» 2 medium plums, peeled and halved

DIRECTIONS

1. In a small saucepan, combine vinegar and brown sugar. Bring to a boil; cook until liquid is reduced by half.

2. On a lightly oiled grill rack, grill peaches, nectarines and plums, covered, over medium heat or broil 4 in. from the heat until tender, 3-4 minutes on each side.

3. Slice the fruit; arrange on a serving plate. Drizzle with sauce.

Grilled Pattypans

INGREDIENTS

» 6 cups pattypan squash (about 1-1/2 pounds)

» 1/4 cup apricot spreadable fruit

» 2 teaspoons hoisin sauce

» 1 teaspoon rice vinegar

» 1/2 teaspoon sesame oil

» 1/4 teaspoon salt

» 1/8 teaspoon ground ginger

DIRECTIONS

1. Place squash in a grill wok or basket coated with cooking spray. Grill, covered, over medium heat until tender, 4 minutes on each side.

2. Meanwhile, in a small bowl, combine the remaining ingredients. Transfer squash to a serving bowl; add sauce and toss gently.

Grilled Pork Tenderloin with Cherry Salsa Mole

Total Time: Prep: 25 min. Grill: 15 min. + standing   Servings: 6

INGREDIENTS

» 2 pork tenderloins (3/4 pound each)

» 1 tablespoon canola oil

» 1/2 teaspoon salt

» 1/4 teaspoon ground cumin

» 1/4 teaspoon chili powder

» 1 cup pitted fresh or frozen dark sweet cherries, thawed, chopped

» 1 jalapeno pepper, seeded and minced

» 1/2 cup finely chopped peeled jicama

» 1 ounce semisweet chocolate, grated

» 2 tablespoons minced fresh cilantro

» 1 green onion, thinly sliced

» 1 tablespoon lime juice

» 1 teaspoon honey

» Salted pumpkin seeds or pepitas

DIRECTIONS

1. Brush tenderloins with oil; sprinkle with salt, cumin and chili powder. Grill, covered, over medium heat until a thermometer reads 145°, 15-20 minutes, turning occasionally. Let stand 10-15 minutes.

2. Meanwhile, combine cherries, jalapeno, jicama, chocolate, cilantro, green onion, lime juice and honey. Slice pork; serve with cherry salsa and pumpkin seeds.

Grilled Veggie Pizza

INGREDIENTS

» 8 small fresh mushrooms, halved

» 1 small zucchini, cut into 1/4-inch slices

» 1 small sweet yellow pepper, sliced

» 1 small sweet red pepper, sliced

» 1 small onion, sliced

» 1 tablespoon white wine vinegar

» 1 tablespoon water

» 4 teaspoons olive oil, divided

» 2 teaspoons minced fresh basil or 1/2 teaspoon dried basil

» 1/4 teaspoon salt

» 1/4 teaspoon pepper

» 1 prebaked 12-inch thin whole wheat pizza crust

» 1 can (8 ounces) pizza sauce

» 2 small tomatoes, chopped

» 2 cups shredded part-skim mozzarella cheese

DIRECTIONS

1. In a large bowl, combine the mushrooms, zucchini, peppers, onion, vinegar, water, 3 teaspoons oil and seasonings. Transfer to a grill wok or basket. Grill, covered, over medium heat for 8-10 minutes or until tender, stirring once.

2. Prepare grill for indirect heat. Brush crust with remaining oil; spread with pizza sauce. Top with grilled vegetables, tomatoes and cheese. Grill, covered, over indirect medium heat for 10-12 minutes or until edges are lightly browned and cheese is melted. Rotate pizza halfway through cooking to ensure evenly browned crust.

Lime and Dill Chimichurri Shrimp

INGREDIENTS

» 1/2 cup extra virgin olive oil

» 1/2 cup packed fresh parsley sprigs

» 1/4 cup snipped fresh dill

» 1/4 cup fresh cilantro leaves

» 3 tablespoons lime juice

» 3 garlic cloves, halved

» 1/2 teaspoon salt

» 1/4 teaspoon pepper

» 1 pound uncooked shrimp (26-30 per pound), peeled and deveined

» 1 medium red onion, cut into thick wedges

» 1 medium zucchini, cut into 1/2-inch pieces

» 1 medium yellow summer squash, cut into 1/2-inch pieces

» 8 cherry tomatoes

» Crusty bread

DIRECTIONS

1. Place first 8 ingredients in a food processor; process until pureed. Reserve 6 tablespoons mixture for serving. Place remaining mixture in a bowl; toss with shrimp and vegetables. Let stand 15 minutes.

2. Alternately thread shrimp and vegetables onto 8 metal or soaked wooden skewers. Grill, covered, over medium heat (or broil 4 in. from heat) until shrimp turn pink, 3-4 minutes per side. Serve on bed of additional herbs, with crusty bread and reserved sauce.

Grilled Italian Sausage Sandwiches

INGREDIENTS

- » 4 large green peppers, thinly sliced
- » 1/2 cup chopped onion
- » 2 tablespoons olive oil
- » 4 garlic cloves, minced
- » 1 can (15 ounces) tomato sauce
- » 1 can (12 ounces) tomato paste
- » 1 cup water
- » 1 tablespoon sugar
- » 2 teaspoons dried basil
- » 1 teaspoon salt
- » 1 teaspoon dried oregano
- » 20 uncooked Italian sausage links
- » 20 sandwich buns
- » Shredded part-skim mozzarella cheese, optional

DIRECTIONS

1. In a large saucepan, saute peppers and onion in oil until crisp-tender. Add garlic; cook 1 minute longer. Drain. Stir in the tomato sauce, tomato paste, water, sugar, basil, salt and oregano. Bring to a boil. Reduce heat; cover and simmer for 30 minutes or until heated through.

2. Meanwhile, grill sausages, covered, over medium heat for 10-16 minutes or until a thermometer reads 160°, turning occasionally. Serve on buns with sauce and cheese if desired.

Spiced Grilled Chicken with Cilantro Butter

INGREDIENTS

» 1 tablespoon chili powder

» 2 teaspoons brown sugar

» 2 teaspoons Gustus Vitae spicy chocolate cinnamon cane sugar

» 1/2 teaspoon salt

» 1/8 teaspoon pepper

» 3 tablespoons olive oil

» 1 tablespoon balsamic vinegar

» 6 bone-in chicken breast halves (8 ounces each)

CILANTRO LIME BUTTER:

» 1/3 cup butter, melted

» 1/4 cup minced fresh cilantro

» 2 tablespoons finely chopped red onion

» 1 tablespoon lime juice

» 1 serrano pepper, finely chopped

» 1/8 teaspoon pepper

DIRECTIONS

1. In a small bowl, combine the first seven ingredients. Brush over chicken.

2. Place chicken skin side down on grill rack. Grill, covered, over indirect medium heat for 15 minutes. Turn; grill 20-25 minutes longer or until a meat thermometer reads 165°.

3. Meanwhile, in a small bowl, combine the butter ingredients. Drizzle over chicken before serving.

Easy Grilled Squash

INGREDIENTS

» 3 tablespoons olive oil

» 2 garlic cloves, minced

» 1/4 teaspoon salt

» 1/4 teaspoon pepper

» 1 small butternut squash, peeled and cut lengthwise
into 1/2-inch slices

DIRECTIONS

1. In a small bowl, combine the oil, garlic, salt and pepper. Brush over squash slices.

2. Grill squash, covered, over medium heat or broil 4 in. from the heat for 4-5 minutes on each side or until tender.

Shrimp 'n' Scallops Tropical Salad

INGREDIENTS

» 2 tablespoons diced peeled mango

» 1 tablespoon diced fresh pineapple

» 1-1/2 teaspoons mango chutney

» 1-1/2 teaspoons olive oil

» 1 teaspoon rice vinegar

» 3/4 teaspoon lime juice

» Dash salt

» Dash crushed red pepper flakes

» 3 cups torn Bibb or Boston lettuce

» 1 cup chopped peeled cucumber

» 1/2 medium ripe avocado, peeled and sliced

» 2 tablespoons coarsely chopped macadamia nuts, toasted

» 1 tablespoon finely chopped red onion

» 1 tablespoon minced fresh cilantro

» 2 tablespoons canola oil

» 1-1/2 teaspoons Caribbean jerk seasoning

» 6 uncooked large shrimp, peeled and deveined

» 6 sea scallops, halved

DIRECTIONS

1. Place the first 8 ingredients in a blender. Cover and process until blended. Divide the lettuce, cucumber, avocado, nuts, onion and cilantro between 2 serving plates.

2. In a small bowl, combine oil and jerk seasoning. Thread shrimp and scallops onto 2 metal or soaked wooden skewers; brush with oil mixture.

3. Grill skewers, covered, over medium heat until shrimp turn pink and scallops are firm and opaque, 2-3 minutes on each side. Place on salads; drizzle with dressing.

Steak Sandwich Kabobs

INGREDIENTS

» 1 pound beef top sirloin steak, cut into 1-inch cubes

» 1 teaspoon steak seasoning

» 1 medium sweet red pepper, cut into 1-inch chunks

» 6 ounces focaccia bread, cut into 1-inch cubes

» 1 medium onion, cut into 1-inch chunks

» 1 tablespoon olive oil

» 3 slices provolone cheese, cut into strips

» 2 cups deli coleslaw

» 1/2 cup chopped walnuts

DIRECTIONS

1. Sprinkle beef with steak seasoning. Alternately thread the beef, red pepper, bread cubes and onion onto 4 metal or soaked wooden skewers; brush with oil.

2. Grill, covered, over medium heat for 8-10 minutes or until meat reaches desired doneness, turning occasionally. For medium-rare, a thermometer should read 135°; medium, 140°; medium-well, 145°. Top with cheese; grill 1-2 minutes longer or until cheese is melted.

3. In a small bowl, combine coleslaw and walnuts. Serve with kabobs.

Cedar Plank Salmon with Blackberry Sauce

INGREDIENTS

» 2 cedar grilling planks

» 2 cups fresh blackberries

» 2 tablespoons white wine

» 1 tablespoon brown sugar

» 1-1/2 teaspoons honey

» 1-1/2 teaspoons chipotle hot pepper sauce

» 1/4 teaspoon salt, divided

» 1/4 teaspoon pepper, divided

» 1/4 cup finely chopped shallots

» 1 garlic clove, minced

» 6 salmon fillets (5 ounces each)

DIRECTIONS

1. Soak grilling planks in water for at least 1 hour.

2. In a food processor, combine the blackberries, wine, brown sugar, honey, hot pepper sauce, 1/8 teaspoon salt and 1/8 teaspoon pepper; cover and process until blended. Strain and discard seeds. Stir shallots and garlic into the sauce; set aside.

3. Place planks on grill over medium-high heat. Cover and heat until planks create a light to medium smoke and begin to crackle, about 3 minutes (this indicates planks are ready). Turn planks over.

4. Sprinkle salmon with remaining salt and pepper. Place on planks. Grill, covered, over medium heat for 12-15 minutes or until fish flakes easily with a fork. Serve with sauce.

Grilled Basil Chicken and Tomatoes

INGREDIENTS

» 3/4 cup balsamic vinegar

» 1/4 cup tightly packed fresh basil leaves

» 2 tablespoons olive oil

» 1 garlic clove, minced

» 1/2 teaspoon salt

» 8 plum tomatoes

» 4 boneless skinless chicken breast halves (4 ounces each)

DIRECTIONS

1. For marinade, place first five ingredients in a blender. Cut 4 tomatoes into quarters and add to blender; cover and process until blended. Halve remaining tomatoes for grilling.

2. In a bowl, combine chicken and 2/3 cup marinade; refrigerate, covered, 1 hour, turning occasionally. Reserve remaining marinade for serving.

3. Drain chicken, discarding marinade. Place chicken on an oiled grill rack over medium heat. Grill chicken, covered, until a thermometer reads 165°, 4-6 minutes per side. Grill tomatoes, covered, over medium heat until lightly browned, 2-4 minutes per side. Serve chicken and tomatoes with reserved marinade.

Grilled Angel Food Cake with Strawberries

INGREDIENTS

» 2 cups sliced fresh strawberries

» 2 teaspoons sugar

» 3 tablespoons butter, melted

» 2 tablespoons balsamic vinegar

» 8 slices angel food cake (about 1 ounce each)

» Optional: Reduced-fat vanilla ice cream and blueberry syrup

DIRECTIONS

1. In a small bowl, toss strawberries with sugar. In another bowl, mix butter and vinegar; brush over cut sides of cake.

2. On a greased rack, grill cake, uncovered, over medium heat until golden brown, 1-2 minutes on each side. Serve cake with strawberries and, if desired, ice cream and blueberry syrup.

Lemony Shrimp & Tomatoes

INGREDIENTS

» 1/3 cup lemon juice

» 2 tablespoons olive oil

» 2 garlic cloves, minced

» 1/2 teaspoon grated lemon zest

» 1 pound uncooked jumbo shrimp, peeled and deveined

» 2/3 cup fresh arugula

» 2 green onions, sliced

» 1/4 cup plain yogurt

» 2 teaspoons 2% milk

» 1 teaspoon cider vinegar

» 1 teaspoon Dijon mustard

» 1/2 teaspoon sugar

» 1/2 teaspoon salt, divided

» 12 cherry tomatoes

» 1/4 teaspoon pepper

DIRECTIONS

1. In a large bowl, whisk lemon juice, oil, garlic and lemon zest until blended. Add shrimp; toss to coat. Let stand 10 minutes.

2. Place arugula, green onions, yogurt, milk, vinegar, mustard, sugar and 1/4 teaspoon salt in a food processor; process until smooth.

3. On 4 metal or soaked wooden skewers, alternately thread shrimp and tomatoes. Sprinkle with pepper and remaining salt.

4. Grill, covered, over medium-high heat or broil 3-4 in. from heat 2-3 minutes on each side or until shrimp are no longer pink. Serve with sauce.

61

Grilled Huli Huli Chicken

INGREDIENTS

» 1 cup packed brown sugar

» 3/4 cup ketchup

» 3/4 cup reduced-sodium soy sauce

» 1/3 cup sherry or chicken broth

» 2-1/2 teaspoons minced fresh gingerroot

» 1-1/2 teaspoons minced garlic

» 24 boneless skinless chicken thighs (about 6 pounds)

DIRECTIONS

1. In a small bowl, mix the first 6 ingredients. Reserve 1-1/3 cups for basting; cover and refrigerate. Divide remaining marinade between 2 large shallow dishes. Add 12 chicken thighs to each; turn to coat. Refrigerate, covered, for 8 hours or overnight.

2. Drain chicken, discarding marinade.

3. Grill chicken, covered, on an oiled rack over medium heat for 6-8 minutes on each side or until a thermometer inserted into chicken reads 170°; baste occasionally with reserved marinade during the last 5 minutes.

Tacos on a Stick

INGREDIENTS

» 1 envelope taco seasoning

» 1 cup tomato juice

» 2 tablespoons canola oil

» 2 pounds beef top sirloin steak, cut into 1-inch cubes

» 1 medium green pepper, cut into chunks

» 1 medium sweet red pepper, cut into chunks

» 1 large onion, cut into wedges

» 16 cherry tomatoes

» Salsa con queso or sour cream, optional

DIRECTIONS

1. In a large shallow dish, combine the taco seasoning, tomato juice and oil; mix well. Remove 1/2 cup for basting; refrigerate. Add beef and turn to coat. Cover; refrigerate for at least 5 hours.

2. Drain and discard marinade from beef. On metal or soaked wooden skewers, alternately thread beef, peppers, onion and tomatoes. Grill, uncovered, over medium heat for 3 minutes on each side. Baste with reserved marinade. Continue turning and basting until meat reaches desired doneness, 8-10 minutes. If desired, serve with salsa con queso or sour cream.

Mango & Grilled Chicken Salad

INGREDIENTS

» 1 pound chicken tenderloins

» 1/2 teaspoon salt

» 1/4 teaspoon pepper

SALAD:

» 6 cups torn mixed salad greens

» 1/4 cup raspberry or balsamic vinaigrette

» 1 medium mango, peeled and cubed

» 1 cup fresh sugar snap peas, halved lengthwise

DIRECTIONS

1. Toss chicken with salt and pepper. On a lightly oiled rack, grill chicken, covered, over medium heat or broil 4 in. from heat on each side until no longer pink, 3-4 minutes. Cut chicken into 1-in. pieces.

2. Divide greens among 4 plates; drizzle with vinaigrette. Top with chicken, mango and peas; serve immediately.

Beef Suya

INGREDIENTS

» 1 cup salted peanuts

» 1 tablespoon paprika

» 2 teaspoons onion powder

» 2 teaspoons ground ginger

» 1 teaspoon crushed red pepper flakes

» 1 teaspoon garlic powder

» 1 beef tri-tip roast or beef top sirloin steak (2 pounds), thinly sliced against the grain

» 2 tablespoons canola oil

» 1 teaspoon salt

» 1 medium onion, cut into wedges

» 1 large tomato, cut into wedges

» Fresh cilantro leaves

DIRECTIONS

1. Place peanuts in a food processor; process until finely chopped. Add paprika, onion powder, ginger, pepper flakes and garlic powder; pulse until combined.

2. Place beef in a large bowl or shallow dish. Drizzle with oil; sprinkle with salt. Toss to coat. Add peanut mixture; turn to coat. Refrigerate, covered, for 2 hours. Drain beef, discarding marinade.

3. Thread beef onto metal or soaked wooden skewers. Grill, covered, over medium-high heat until beef reaches desired doneness, 10-15 minutes, turning occasionally. Serve with onion, tomato and cilantro.

Grilled Vegetable Platter

Total Time: Prep: 20 min. + marinating Grill: 10 min.   Servings: 6

INGREDIENTS

» 1/4 cup olive oil

» 2 tablespoons honey

» 4 teaspoons balsamic vinegar

» 1 teaspoon dried oregano

» 1/2 teaspoon garlic powder

» 1/8 teaspoon pepper

» Dash salt

» 1 pound fresh asparagus, trimmed

» 3 small carrots, cut in half lengthwise

» 1 large sweet red pepper, cut into 1-inch strips

» 1 medium yellow summer squash, cut into 1/2-inch slices

» 1 medium red onion, cut into wedges

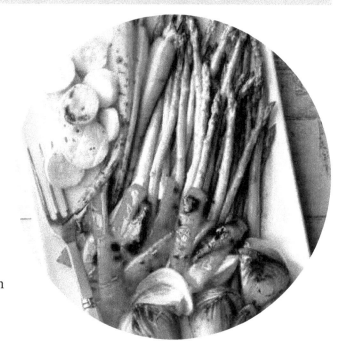

DIRECTIONS

1. In a small bowl, whisk the first 7 ingredients. Place 3 tablespoons marinade in a large bowl. Add vegetables; turn to coat. Cover; marinate 1-1/2 hours at room temperature.

2. Transfer vegetables to a grilling grid; place grid on grill rack. Grill vegetables, covered, over medium heat until crisp-tender, 8-12 minutes, turning occasionally.

3. Place vegetables on a large serving plate. Drizzle with remaining marinade.

Cola Burgers

INGREDIENTS

» 1 large egg

» 1/2 cup cola, divided

» 1/2 cup crushed saltines (about 15)

» 6 tablespoons French salad dressing, divided

» 2 tablespoons grated Parmesan cheese

» 1/4 teaspoon salt

» 1-1/2 pounds ground beef

» 6 hamburger buns, split

» Optional toppings: Lettuce leaves, sliced tomato, sliced red onion, pickles and sliced cheese

DIRECTIONS

1. In a large bowl, combine egg, 1/4 cup cola, cracker crumbs, 2 tablespoons salad dressing, Parmesan cheese and salt. Crumble beef over mixture and mix well. Shape into six 3/4-in.-thick patties (mixture will be moist).

2. In a small bowl, combine remaining cola and salad dressing; set aside.

3. Grill burgers, covered, over medium heat for 3 minutes on each side. Brush with cola mixture. Continue grilling until a thermometer reads 160°, 6-8 minutes, brushing and turning occasionally. Serve on buns. Serve burgers with optional toppings as desired.

Grilled Honey-Balsamic Glazed Fruit

INGREDIENTS

» 1/2 cup balsamic vinegar

» 1/2 cup honey

» Dash salt

» 6 medium peaches or nectarines, halved and pitted

» Vanilla ice cream, optional

DIRECTIONS

1. In a small saucepan, combine vinegar, honey and salt; cook and stir over low heat until blended, 2-3 minutes. Reserve 1/3 cup mixture for brushing peaches.

2. Bring remaining mixture to a boil over medium heat; cook and stir just until mixture begins to thicken slightly (do not overcook), 4-6 minutes. Remove from heat.

3. Brush peaches with some of the reserved balsamic mixture. Grill, covered, on an greased rack over medium heat until caramelized, brushing occasionally with remaining reserved balsamic mixture, 6-8 minutes on each side. Serve with glaze and, if desired, ice cream.

Easy Marinated Grilled Flank Steak

INGREDIENTS
» 1 cup barbecue sauce

» 1/2 cup burgundy wine or beef broth

» 1/4 cup lemon juice

» 1 beef flank steak (2 pounds)

DIRECTIONS

1. In a small bowl, whisk barbecue sauce, wine and lemon juice until blended. Pour 1 cup marinade into a shallow dish. Add beef and turn to coat. Cover; refrigerate 4 hours or overnight. Cover and refrigerate remaining marinade.

2. Drain beef, discarding marinade in dish. Grill steak, covered, over medium heat until meat reaches desired doneness (for medium-rare, a thermometer should read 135°; medium, 140°; medium-well, 145°), 6-8 minutes on each side. Let stand 5 minutes before thinly slicing across the grain. Serve with reserved marinade.

Barbecued Chicken Pizzas

Total Time: Prep: 25 min. Grill: 10 min.   Servings: 2

INGREDIENTS

» 2 boneless skinless chicken breast halves (6 ounces each)

» 1/4 teaspoon pepper

» 1 cup barbecue sauce, divided

» 1 tube (13.8 ounces) refrigerated pizza crust

» 2 teaspoons olive oil

» 2 cups shredded Gouda cheese

» 1 small red onion, halved and thinly sliced

» 1/4 cup minced fresh cilantro

DIRECTIONS

1. Sprinkle chicken with pepper; place on an oiled grill rack over medium heat. Grill, covered, until a thermometer reads 165°, 5-7 minutes per side, basting frequently with 1/2 cup barbecue sauce during the last 4 minutes. Cool slightly. Cut into cubes.

2. Divide dough in half. On a well-greased large sheet of heavy-duty foil, press each portion of dough into a 10x8-in. rectangle; brush lightly with oil. Invert dough onto grill rack; peel off foil. Grill, covered, over medium heat until bottom is lightly browned, 1-2 minutes.

3. Remove from grill. Spread grilled sides with remaining barbecue sauce. Top with cheese, chicken and onion. Grill, covered, until bottom is lightly browned and cheese is melted, 2-3 minutes. Sprinkle with cilantro.

Grilled Chicken and Mango Skewers

INGREDIENTS

» 3 medium ears sweet corn

» 1 tablespoon butter

» 1/3 cup plus 3 tablespoons sliced green onions, divided

» 1 pound boneless skinless chicken breasts, cut into 1-inch cubes

» 1/2 teaspoon salt

» 1/4 teaspoon pepper

» 1 medium mango, peeled and cut into 1-inch cubes

» 1 tablespoon extra virgin olive oil

» Lime wedges, optional

DIRECTIONS

1. Cut corn from cobs. In a large skillet, heat butter over medium-high heat; saute cut corn until crisp-tender, about 5 minutes. Stir in 1/3 cup green onions. Keep warm.

2. Toss chicken with salt and pepper. Alternately thread chicken and mango onto 4 metal or soaked wooden skewers. Brush with oil.

3. Grill, covered, over medium heat or broil 4 in. from heat until chicken is no longer pink, 10-12 minutes, turning occasionally. Serve with corn mixture; sprinkle with remaining green onions. If desired, serve with lime wedges.

Fresh Artichokes with Lemon-Yogurt Dip

INGREDIENTS

» 6 medium artichokes

» 3 tablespoons olive oil

» Sea salt and coarsely ground pepper to taste

» 1-1/2 cups plain yogurt

» 1 teaspoon lemon juice

» 1/4 teaspoon salt

» 1/4 teaspoon pepper

» Lemon wedges

DIRECTIONS

1. Using a sharp knife, cut 1 in. from top of each artichoke and trim stem so it will stand upright. Using kitchen scissors, cut off tips of outer leaves. Place artichokes upright in a Dutch oven; cover with water and bring to a boil. Reduce heat; simmer, covered, until a leaf in the center pulls out easily, 35-40 minutes. Invert artichokes to drain. Cool slightly; cut each in half lengthwise. With a spoon, carefully scrape and remove fuzzy center of artichokes.

2. In a cast-iron skillet or grill pan, heat oil over medium-high heat. Place artichokes in pan, cut side down. Cook until lightly browned, 5-7 minutes. Sprinkle with salt and pepper. In a small bowl, mix yogurt, lemon juice, salt and pepper. Serve with artichokes and lemon wedges.

Grilled Peach, Rice & Arugula Salad

INGREDIENTS

» 3 tablespoons cider vinegar

» 2 tablespoons Dijon mustard

» 2 tablespoons canola oil

» 2 tablespoons maple syrup

» 1 tablespoon finely chopped shallot

» 1/4 teaspoon cayenne pepper

SALAD:

» 1 package (8.8 ounces) ready-to-serve long grain and wild rice

» 2 medium peaches, quartered

» 6 cups fresh arugula (about 4 ounces)

» 6 bacon strips, cooked and crumbled

» 1/2 cup crumbled goat cheese

DIRECTIONS

1. For dressing, whisk together first 6 ingredients.

2. Prepare rice according to package directions; cool slightly. Place peaches on a lightly oiled grill rack over medium heat. Grill, covered, until lightly browned, 6-8 minutes, turning occasionally.

3. To serve, add bacon and 1/4 cup dressing to rice. Line a platter with arugula; top with rice mixture and peaches. Drizzle with remaining dressing; top with cheese.

Hawaiian Beef Sliders

INGREDIENTS

» 1 can (20 ounces) unsweetened crushed pineapple

» 1 teaspoon pepper

» 1/4 teaspoon salt

» 1-1/2 pounds lean ground beef (90% lean)

» 1/4 cup reduced-sodium soy sauce

» 2 tablespoons ketchup

» 1 tablespoon white vinegar

» 2 garlic cloves, minced

» 1/4 teaspoon crushed red pepper flakes

» 18 miniature whole wheat buns

» Baby spinach leaves

» 3 center-cut bacon strips, cooked and crumbled

» Sliced jalapeno peppers, optional

DIRECTIONS

1. Drain pineapple, reserving juice and 1-1/2 cups pineapple (save the extra pineapple for another use). In a large bowl, combine 3/4 cup reserved crushed pineapple, pepper and salt. Crumble beef over mixture and mix lightly but thoroughly. Shape into 18 patties; place in two 11x7-in. dishes.

2. In a small bowl, combine soy sauce, ketchup, vinegar, garlic, pepper flakes and reserved pineapple juice. Pour half the marinade into each dish; cover and refrigerate 1 hour, turning once.

3. Drain and discard marinade. On a lightly oiled grill, grill patties, covered, over medium heat or broil 4 in. from heat. Grill or broil until a thermometer reads 160° and juices run clear, 4-5 minutes on each side.

4. Grill buns, uncovered, until toasted, 1-2 minutes. Serve burgers on buns with spinach, remaining pineapple, bacon and, if desired, jalapeno peppers.

Ginger Salmon with Cucumber Lime Sauce

INGREDIENTS

» 1 tablespoon grated lime zest

» 1/4 cup lime juice

» 2 tablespoons olive oil

» 2 tablespoons rice vinegar or white wine vinegar

» 4 teaspoons sugar

» 1/2 teaspoon salt

» 1/2 teaspoon ground coriander

» 1/2 teaspoon freshly ground pepper

» 1/3 cup chopped fresh cilantro

» 1 tablespoon finely chopped onion

» 2 teaspoons minced fresh gingerroot

» 2 garlic cloves, minced

» 2 medium cucumbers, peeled, seeded and chopped

SALMON:

» 1/3 cup minced fresh gingerroot

» 1 tablespoon lime juice

» 1 tablespoon olive oil

» 1/2 teaspoon salt

» 1/2 teaspoon freshly ground pepper

» 10 salmon fillets (6 ounces each)

DIRECTIONS

1. Place the first 13 ingredients in a blender. Cover and process until pureed.

2. In a small bowl, mix ginger, lime juice, oil, salt and pepper. Rub over flesh side of salmon fillets.

3. Lightly oil the grill rack. Place salmon on rack, skin side down. Grill, covered, over medium-high heat 10-12 minutes or until fish just begins to flake easily with a fork. Serve with sauce.

75

Beef and Blue Cheese Penne with Pesto

Total Time: Prep/Total Time: 30 min.   Servings: 4

INGREDIENTS

» 2 cups uncooked whole wheat penne pasta

» 2 beef tenderloin steaks (6 ounces each)

» 1/4 teaspoon salt

» 1/4 teaspoon pepper

» 5 ounces fresh baby spinach (about 6 cups), coarsely chopped

» 2 cups grape tomatoes, halved

» 1/3 cup prepared pesto

» 1/4 cup chopped walnuts

» 1/4 cup crumbled Gorgonzola cheese

DIRECTIONS

1. Cook pasta according to package directions.

2. Meanwhile, sprinkle steaks with salt and pepper. Grill steaks, covered, over medium heat or broil 4 in. from heat 5-7 minutes on each side or until meat reaches desired doneness (for medium-rare, a thermometer should read 135°; medium, 140°; medium-well, 145°).

3. Drain pasta; transfer to a large bowl. Add spinach, tomatoes, pesto and walnuts; toss to coat. Cut steak into thin slices. Serve pasta mixture with beef; sprinkle with cheese.

Grilled Figgy Pies

INGREDIENTS

» 2 sheets refrigerated pie crust

» 12 dried figs

» 1/4 cup bourbon

» 1/2 cup chopped walnuts

» 1/4 cup plus 1 tablespoon maple syrup, divided

» 1 teaspoon ground cinnamon

» 1/2 teaspoon ground nutmeg

» 1/2 teaspoon vanilla extract

» 2/3 cup (about 5 ounces) mascarpone cheese

» 1 large egg

» 1 tablespoon water

DIRECTIONS

1. Warm pie crust to room temperature according to package directions. Meanwhile, in a small saucepan, combine figs and bourbon; add enough water to cover by 1 in. Cook, covered, over low heat until figs are plump, 15-20 minutes. Remove from heat; drain. Cool 15 minutes and pat dry. Cut each fig into quarters. Set aside.

2. In same saucepan over medium-low heat, combine walnuts with 1/4 cup maple syrup, cinnamon and nutmeg. Cook, stirring constantly, until liquid is almost evaporated, 5-7 minutes. Spread nuts on a baking sheet lined with parchment; freeze until set, about 10 minutes.

3. Unroll pie crusts. Using a 4-in. round cutter, cut 12 circles, rolling and cutting scraps as necessary. Stir vanilla and remaining 1 Tbsp. maple syrup into mascarpone cheese. Spread scant 1 tablespoon mascarpone mixture over half of each circle to within 1/4 in. of edge; layer with 2 teaspoons maple walnuts and 4 fig pieces. Make an egg wash by whisking egg and water; use to moisten edge of crust. Fold crust over filling; press edges with a fork to seal. Repeat with remaining crust and filling. Brush egg wash over pies. Freeze pies on a parchment-lined baking sheet 10 minutes.

4. Remove from baking sheet. Grill pies, covered, on a well-greased grill rack over medium direct heat until golden brown, 5-7 minutes per side.

INGREDIENTS

» 1 large red onion, sliced

» 1 cup minced fresh cilantro

» 1/4 cup white wine vinegar

» 1/4 cup Key lime juice

» 3 tablespoons extra virgin olive oil, divided

» 6 Key limes, halved

» 1 beef flank steak (1 pound)

» 1 teaspoon kosher salt

» 1/8 teaspoon pepper

DIRECTIONS

1. In a small bowl, combine onion, cilantro, vinegar, lime juice and 2 tablespoons oil until blended. Pour 1 cup marinade into a large bowl or shallow dish. Add lime halves. Rub steak with remaining oil; sprinkle with salt and pepper. Add to bowl; turn to coat. Refrigerate 8 hours or overnight. Cover and refrigerate remaining marinade.

2. Drain steak, discarding marinade and limes in bowl. Place reserved marinade in a food processor; process until chopped.

3. Grill steak, covered, over medium heat or broil 4 in. from heat until meat reaches desired doneness (for medium-rare, a thermometer should read 135°; medium, 140°), 6-8 minutes per side. Baste occasionally with reserved marinade. Let stand 10 minutes before thinly slicing steak across the grain.

Bacon & Swiss Chicken Sandwiches

Total Time: Prep/Total Time: 25 min.   Servings: 4

INGREDIENTS

» 1/4 cup reduced-fat mayonnaise

» 1 tablespoon Dijon mustard

» 1 tablespoon honey

» 4 boneless skinless chicken breast halves (4 ounces each)

» 1/2 teaspoon Montreal steak seasoning

» 4 slices Swiss cheese

» 4 whole wheat hamburger buns, split

» 2 bacon strips, cooked and crumbled

» Lettuce leaves and tomato slices, optional

DIRECTIONS

1. In a small bowl, mix mayonnaise, mustard and honey. Pound chicken with a meat mallet to 1/2-in. thickness. Sprinkle chicken with steak seasoning. Grill chicken, covered, over medium heat or broil 4 in. from heat until a thermometer reads 165°, 4-6 minutes on each side Top with cheese during the last 1 minute of cooking.

2. Grill buns over medium heat, cut side down, until toasted, 30-60 seconds. Serve chicken on buns with bacon, mayonnaise mixture and, if desired, lettuce and tomato.

Grilled Brussels Sprouts

INGREDIENTS

» 16 fresh Brussels sprouts (about 1-1/2-inch diameter), trimmed

» 1 medium sweet red pepper

» 1 medium onion

» 1/2 teaspoon salt

» 1/2 teaspoon garlic powder

» 1/4 teaspoon coarsely ground pepper

» 1 tablespoon olive oil

DIRECTIONS

1. In a large saucepan, place a steamer basket over 1 in. of water. Bring water to a boil. Place Brussels sprouts in basket. Reduce heat to maintain a simmer; steam, covered, until crisp-tender, 4-6 minutes. Cool slightly; cut each sprout in half.

2. Cut red pepper and onion into 1-1/2-in. pieces. On 4 metal or soaked wooden skewers, alternately thread Brussels sprouts, red pepper and onion. Mix salt, garlic powder and pepper. Brush vegetables with oil; sprinkle with salt mixture. Grill, covered, over medium heat or broil 4 in. from heat until vegetables are tender, 10-12 minutes, turning occasionally.

Cake & Berry Campfire Cobbler

INGREDIENTS

» 2 cans (21 ounces each) raspberry pie filling

» 1 package yellow cake mix (regular size)

» 1-1/4 cups water

» 1/2 cup canola oil

» Vanilla ice cream, optional

DIRECTIONS

1. Prepare grill or campfire for low heat, using 16-20 charcoal briquettes or large wood chips.

2. Line an ovenproof Dutch oven with heavy-duty aluminum foil; add pie filling. In a large bowl, combine the cake mix, water and oil. Spread over pie filling.

3. Cover Dutch oven. When briquettes or wood chips are covered with white ash, place Dutch oven directly on top of 8-10 of them. Using long-handled tongs, place remaining briquettes on pan cover.

4. Cook until filling is bubbly and a toothpick inserted in the topping comes out clean, 30-40 minutes. To check for doneness, use the tongs to carefully lift the cover. If desired, serve with ice cream.

Chicken Skewers with Cool Avocado Sauce

INGREDIENTS

» 1 pound boneless skinless chicken breasts

» 1/2 cup lime juice

» 1 tablespoon balsamic vinegar

» 2 teaspoons minced chipotle pepper in adobo sauce

» 1/2 teaspoon salt

» SAUCE:

» 1 medium ripe avocado, peeled and pitted

» 1/2 cup fat-free sour cream

» 2 tablespoons minced fresh cilantro

» 2 teaspoons lime juice

» 1 teaspoon grated lime zest

» 1/4 teaspoon salt

DIRECTIONS

1. Flatten chicken to 1/4-in. thickness; cut lengthwise into sixteen 1-in.-wide strips. In a large bowl, combine the lime juice, vinegar, chipotle pepper and salt; add the chicken and turn to coat. Cover and refrigerate for 30 minutes.

2. Meanwhile, for the sauce, place remaining ingredients in a food processor; cover and process until blended. Transfer to a serving bowl; cover and refrigerate until serving.

3. Drain chicken, discarding marinade. Thread meat onto 4 metal or soaked wooden skewers. On a lightly oiled rack, grill skewers, covered, over medium heat (or broil 4 in. from the heat) for 8-12 minutes or until no longer pink, turning frequently. Serve with sauce.

California Burger Bowls

INGREDIENTS

» 3 tablespoons fat-free milk

» 2 tablespoons quick-cooking oats

» 3/4 teaspoon salt

» 1/2 teaspoon ground cumin

» 1/2 teaspoon chili powder

» 1/2 teaspoon pepper

» 1 pound lean ground turkey

» 4 cups baby kale salad blend

» 1-1/2 cups cubed fresh pineapple (1/2 inch)

» 1 medium mango, peeled and thinly sliced

» 1 medium ripe avocado, peeled and thinly sliced

» 1 medium sweet red pepper, cut into strips

» 4 tomatillos, husks removed, thinly sliced

» 1/4 cup reduced-fat chipotle mayonnaise

DIRECTIONS

1. In a large bowl, mix milk, oats and seasonings. Add turkey; mix lightly but thoroughly. Shape into four 1/2-in.-thick patties.

2. Place burgers on an oiled grill rack over medium heat. Grill, covered, until a thermometer reads 165°, 4-5 minutes per side. Serve over salad blend, along with remaining ingredients.

Grilled Sausage-Basil Pizzas

Total Time: Prep/Total Time: 30 min.   Servings: 4

INGREDIENTS

» 4 Italian sausage links (4 ounces each)

» 4 naan flatbreads or whole pita breads

» 1/4 cup olive oil

» 1 cup tomato basil pasta sauce

» 2 cups shredded part-skim mozzarella cheese

» 1/2 cup grated Parmesan cheese

» 1/2 cup thinly sliced fresh basil

DIRECTIONS

1. Grill sausages, covered, over medium heat until a thermometer reads 160°, 10-12 minutes, turning occasionally. Cut into 1/4-in. slices.

2. Brush both sides of flatbreads with oil. Grill flatbreads, covered, over medium heat until bottoms are lightly browned, 2-3 minutes.

3. Remove from grill. Layer grilled sides with sauce, sausage, cheeses and basil. Return to grill; cook, covered, until cheese is melted, 2-3 minutes longer.

Grilled Jerk Shrimp Orzo Salad

INGREDIENTS

» 1/3 cup uncooked whole wheat orzo pasta

» 1/2 pound uncooked shrimp (31-40 per pound), peeled and deveined

» 1 tablespoon Caribbean jerk seasoning

» 1 medium ear sweet corn, husked

» 1 teaspoon olive oil

» 6 fresh asparagus spears, trimmed

» 1 small sweet red pepper, chopped

DRESSING:

» 3 tablespoons lime juice

» 1 tablespoon water

» 1 tablespoon olive oil

» 1/8 teaspoon salt

» 1/8 teaspoon pepper

DIRECTIONS

1. Cook orzo according to package directions. Rinse with cold water; drain well. Meanwhile, toss shrimp with jerk seasoning; thread onto metal or soaked wooden skewers. Brush corn with oil.

2. On a covered grill over medium heat, cook corn until tender and lightly browned, 10-12 minutes, turning occasionally; cook asparagus until crisp-tender, 5-7 minutes, turning occasionally. Grill shrimp until they turn pink, 1-2 minutes per side.

3. Cut corn from cob; cut asparagus into 1-in. pieces. Remove shrimp from skewers. In a large bowl, combine orzo, grilled vegetables, shrimp and red pepper. Whisk together dressing ingredients; toss with salad.

Tarragon Asparagus

INGREDIENTS

» 2 pounds fresh asparagus, trimmed

» 2 tablespoons olive oil

» 1 teaspoon salt

» 1/2 teaspoon pepper

» 1/4 cup honey

» 2 to 4 tablespoons minced fresh tarragon

DIRECTIONS

1. On a large plate, toss asparagus with oil, salt and pepper. Grill, covered, over medium heat 6-8 minutes or until crisp-tender, turning occasionally and basting frequently with honey during the last 3 minutes. Sprinkle with tarragon.

Honey Chipotle Ribs

INGREDIENTS

» 6 pounds pork baby back ribs

BARBECUE SAUCE:

» 3 cups ketchup

» 2 bottles (11.2 ounces each) Guinness beer

» 2 cups barbecue sauce

» 2/3 cup honey

» 1 small onion, chopped

» 1/4 cup Worcestershire sauce

» 2 tablespoons Dijon mustard

» 2 tablespoons chopped chipotle peppers in adobo

sauce

» 4 teaspoons ground chipotle pepper

» 1 teaspoon salt

» 1 teaspoon garlic powder

» 1/2 teaspoon pepper

DIRECTIONS

1. Wrap ribs in large pieces of heavy-duty foil; seal edges of foil. Grill, covered, over indirect medium heat for 1 to 1-1/2 hours or until tender.

2. In a large saucepan, combine sauce ingredients; bring to a boil. Reduce heat; simmer, uncovered, for about 45 minutes or until thickened, stirring occasionally.

3. Carefully remove ribs from foil. Place over direct heat; baste with some of the sauce. Grill, covered, over medium heat for about 30 minutes or until browned, turning once and basting occasionally with additional sauce. Serve with remaining sauce.

Stuffed Grilled Zucchini

INGREDIENTS

» 4 medium zucchini

» 5 teaspoons olive oil, divided

» 2 tablespoons finely chopped red onion

» 1/4 teaspoon minced garlic

» 1/2 cup dry bread crumbs

» 1/2 cup shredded part-skim mozzarella cheese

» 1 tablespoon minced fresh mint

» 1/2 teaspoon salt

» 3 tablespoons grated Parmesan cheese

DIRECTIONS

1. Cut zucchini in half lengthwise; scoop out flesh, leaving 1/4-in. shells. Brush with 2 teaspoons oil; set aside. Chop zucchini flesh.

2. In a large skillet, saute flesh and onion in remaining oil. Add garlic; cook 1 minute longer. Add bread crumbs; cook and stir until golden brown, about 2 minutes.

3. Remove from the heat. Stir in the mozzarella cheese, mint and salt. Spoon into zucchini shells. Sprinkle with Parmesan cheese.

4. Grill, covered, over medium heat until zucchini is tender, 8-10 minutes.

Tomato, Avocado and Grilled Corn Salad

INGREDIENTS

» 1 medium ear sweet corn, husks removed

» 3 large red tomatoes, sliced

» 3 large yellow tomatoes, sliced

» 3/4 teaspoon kosher salt, divided

» 1/2 teaspoon pepper, divided

» 2 medium ripe avocados, peeled and sliced

» 1/4 cup olive oil

» 2 tablespoons red wine vinegar

» 1 tablespoon minced fresh basil, plus more for garnish

» 1/3 cup crumbled feta cheese

DIRECTIONS

1. Grill corn, covered, over medium heat 10-12 minutes or until lightly browned and tender, turning occasionally. Cool slightly. Cut corn from cob.

2. Arrange tomato slices on a large serving platter. Sprinkle with 1/2 teaspoon salt and 1/4 teaspoon pepper. Top with avocado slices. Whisk together the oil, vinegar, basil and remaining salt and pepper; drizzle half over the tomatoes and avocado. Top with grilled corn and feta; drizzle remaining dressing over top. Garnish with additional chopped basil.

Chicken Alfredo with Grilled Apples

Total Time: Prep/Total Time: 25 min.   Servings: 4

INGREDIENTS

» 4 boneless skinless chicken breast halves (6 ounces each)

» 4 teaspoons chicken seasoning

» 1 large Braeburn or Gala apple, cut into 1/2-inch wedges

» 1 tablespoon lemon juice

» 4 slices provolone cheese

» 1/2 cup Alfredo sauce, warmed

» 1/4 cup crumbled blue cheese

DIRECTIONS

1. Sprinkle both sides of chicken with chicken seasoning. In a small bowl, toss apple wedges with lemon juice.

2. Place chicken on an oiled grill rack. Grill chicken, covered, over medium heat 5-8 minutes on each side or until a thermometer reads 165°. Grill apple, covered, over medium heat 2-3 minutes on each side or until lightly browned. Top chicken with provolone cheese; cook, covered, 1-2 minutes longer or until cheese is melted.

3. Serve chicken with Alfredo sauce and apple. Sprinkle with blue cheese.

Sweet Sriracha Wings

INGREDIENTS

» 12 chicken wings (about 3 pounds)

» 1 tablespoon canola oil

» 2 teaspoons ground coriander

» 1/2 teaspoon garlic salt

» 1/4 teaspoon pepper

SAUCE:

» 1/4 cup butter, cubed

» 1/2 cup orange juice

» 1/3 cup Sriracha chili sauce

» 3 tablespoons honey

» 2 tablespoons lime juice

» 1/4 cup chopped fresh cilantro

DIRECTIONS

1. Place chicken wings in a large bowl. Mix oil, coriander, garlic salt and pepper; add to wings and toss to coat. Refrigerate, covered, 2 hours or overnight.

2. For sauce, in a small saucepan, melt butter. Stir in orange juice, chili sauce, honey and lime juice until blended.

3. Grill wings, covered, over medium heat 15-18 minutes or until juices run clear, turning occasionally; brush with some of the sauce during the last 5 minutes of grilling.

4. Transfer chicken to a large bowl; add remaining sauce and toss to coat. Sprinkle with cilantro.

Cilantro Lime Shrimp

INGREDIENTS

» 1/3 cup chopped fresh cilantro

» 1-1/2 teaspoons grated lime zest

» 1/3 cup lime juice

» 1 jalapeno pepper, seeded and minced

» 2 tablespoons olive oil

» 3 garlic cloves, minced

» 1/4 teaspoon salt

» 1/4 teaspoon ground cumin

» 1/4 teaspoon pepper

» 1 pound uncooked shrimp (16-20 per pound), peeled and deveined

» Lime slices

DIRECTIONS

1. Mix first 9 ingredients; toss with shrimp. Let stand 15 minutes.

2. Thread shrimp and lime slices onto 4 metal or soaked wooden skewers. Grill, covered, over medium heat until shrimp turn pink, 2-4 minutes per side.

Honey-Mustard Brats

INGREDIENTS

» 1/4 cup Dijon mustard

» 1/4 cup honey

» 2 tablespoons mayonnaise

» 1 teaspoon steak sauce

» 4 uncooked bratwurst links

» 4 brat buns, split

DIRECTIONS

1. In a small bowl, mix mustard, honey, mayonnaise and steak sauce.

2. Grill bratwurst, covered, over medium heat 15-20 minutes or until a thermometer reads 160°, turning occasionally; brush frequently with mustard mixture during the last 5 minutes. Serve on buns.

INGREDIENTS

» 1 pound plum tomatoes (about 6), seeded and chopped

» 1 cup chopped celery or fennel bulb

» 1/4 cup minced fresh basil

» 3 tablespoons balsamic vinegar

» 3 tablespoons olive oil

» 3 tablespoons Dijon mustard

» 2 garlic cloves, minced

» 1/2 teaspoon salt

MAYONNAISE SPREAD:

» 1/2 cup mayonnaise

» 1/4 cup Dijon mustard

» 1 tablespoon finely chopped green onion

» 1 garlic clove, minced

» 3/4 teaspoon dried oregano

» 1 loaf (1 pound) French bread, cut into 1/2-inch slices

DIRECTIONS

1. In a large bowl, combine the first eight ingredients. Cover and refrigerate for at least 30 minutes. For mayonnaise spread, in a small bowl, combine the mayonnaise, mustard, onion, garlic and oregano; set aside.

2. Grill bread slices, uncovered, over medium-low heat for 1-2 minutes or until lightly toasted. Turn bread; spread with mayonnaise mixture. Grill 1-2 minutes longer or until bottoms of bread is toasted. Drain tomato mixture; spoon over tops.

Lemon Garlic Mushrooms

INGREDIENTS

» 1/4 cup lemon juice

» 3 tablespoons minced fresh parsley

» 2 tablespoons olive oil

» 3 garlic cloves, minced

» Pepper to taste

» 1 pound large fresh mushrooms

DIRECTIONS

1. For dressing, whisk together first 5 ingredients. Toss mushrooms with 2 tablespoons dressing.

2. Grill mushrooms, covered, over medium-high heat until tender, 5-7 minutes per side. Toss with remaining dressing before serving.

Total Time: Prep/Total Time: 30 min.   Servings: 4

INGREDIENTS

» 4 ears fresh sweet corn

» 2 jalapeno peppers

» 3 tablespoons canola oil, divided

» 3/4 teaspoon salt, divided

» 1/4 cup panko bread crumbs

» 1/2 teaspoon smoked paprika

» 1/2 teaspoon dried Mexican oregano

» 4 ounces cream cheese, softened

» 1/4 cup media crema table cream or sour cream thinned with 1 teaspoon 2% milk

» 2 tablespoons lime juice

» Ground chipotle pepper or chili powder

» Optional: Chopped fresh cilantro and lime wedges

DIRECTIONS

1. Husk corn. Rub corn and jalapenos with 2 tablespoons canola oil. Grill, covered, on a greased grill rack over medium-high direct heat until lightly charred on all sides, 10-12 minutes. Remove from heat. When jalapenos are cool enough to handle, remove skin, seeds and membranes; chop finely. Set aside.

2. Sprinkle corn with 1/2 teaspoon salt. In a small skillet, heat remaining oil over medium heat. Add panko; cook and stir until starting to brown. Add paprika and oregano; cook until crumbs are toasted and fragrant.

3. Meanwhile, combine cream cheese, crema, lime juice and remaining salt; spread over corn. Sprinkle with bread crumbs, jalapenos and chipotle pepper. If desired, sprinkle with cilantro and serve with lime wedges.

Crab & Shrimp Stuffed Sole

INGREDIENTS

» 1 can (6 ounces) crabmeat, drained, flaked and cartilage removed

» 1/2 cup chopped cooked peeled shrimp

» 1/4 cup soft bread crumbs

» 1/4 cup butter, melted, divided

» 2 tablespoons whipped cream cheese

» 2 teaspoons minced chives

» 1 garlic clove, minced

» 1 teaspoon grated lemon zest

» 1 teaspoon minced fresh parsley

» 4 sole fillets (6 ounces each)

» 1-1/2 cups cherry tomatoes

» 2 tablespoons dry white wine or chicken broth

» 2 tablespoons lemon juice

» 1/2 teaspoon salt

» 1/2 teaspoon pepper

DIRECTIONS

1. In a small bowl, combine the crab, shrimp, bread crumbs, 2 tablespoons butter, cream cheese, chives, garlic, lemon zest and parsley. Spoon about 1/4 cup stuffing onto each fillet; roll up and secure with toothpicks.

2. Place each fillet on a double thickness of heavy-duty foil (about 18x12 in.). Combine the tomatoes, wine, lemon juice, salt, pepper and remaining butter; spoon over fillets. Fold foil around fish and seal tightly.

3. Grill, covered, over medium heat for 12-15 minutes or until fish flakes easily with a fork. Open foil carefully to allow steam to escape.

Grilled Chicken Salad with Blueberry Vinaigrette

INGREDIENTS

» 2 boneless skinless chicken breast halves (6 ounces each)

» 1 tablespoon olive oil

» 1 garlic clove, minced

» 1/4 teaspoon salt

» 1/4 teaspoon pepper

» VINAIGRETTE:

» 1/4 cup olive oil

» 1/4 cup blueberry preserves

» 2 tablespoons balsamic vinegar

» 2 tablespoons maple syrup

» 1/4 teaspoon ground mustard

» 1/8 teaspoon salt

» Dash pepper

SALADS:

» 1 package (10 ounces) ready-to-serve salad greens

» 1 cup fresh blueberries

» 1/2 cup canned mandarin oranges

» 1 cup crumbled goat cheese

DIRECTIONS

1. Toss chicken with oil, garlic, salt and pepper; refrigerate, covered, 30 minutes. In a small bowl, whisk together vinaigrette ingredients; refrigerate, covered, until serving.

2. Grill chicken, covered, over medium heat until a thermometer reads 165°, 5-7 minutes per side. Let stand 5 minutes before slicing.

3. Place greens on a serving plate; top with chicken, blueberries and mandarin oranges. Whisk vinaigrette again; drizzle over salad. Top with cheese.

Grilled Cabbage

INGREDIENTS

» 1 medium head cabbage (about 1-1/2 pounds)

» 1/3 cup butter, softened

» 1/4 cup chopped onion

» 1/2 teaspoon garlic salt

» 1/4 teaspoon pepper

DIRECTIONS

1. Cut cabbage into 8 wedges; place on a double thickness of heavy-duty foil (about 24x12 in.). Spread cut sides with butter. Sprinkle with onion, garlic salt and pepper.

2. Fold foil around cabbage and seal tightly. Grill, covered, over medium heat until tender, about 20 minutes. Open foil carefully to allow steam to escape.

Grilled Southwestern Potato Salad

INGREDIENTS

» 1-1/2 pounds large red potatoes, quartered lengthwise

» 3 tablespoons olive oil

» 2 poblano peppers

» 2 medium ears sweet corn, husks removed

» 1/2 cup buttermilk

» 1/2 cup sour cream

» 1 tablespoon lime juice

» 1 jalapeno pepper, seeded and minced

» 1 tablespoon minced fresh cilantro

» 1-1/2 teaspoons garlic salt

» 1 teaspoon ground cumin

» 1/4 to 1/2 teaspoon cayenne pepper

» Lime wedges

DIRECTIONS

1. Place potatoes in a large saucepan; add water to cover. Bring to a boil. Reduce heat; cook, uncovered, 5 minutes. Drain potatoes and toss with oil.

2. Grill poblanos, covered, over high heat 8-10 minutes or until skins are blistered and blackened on all sides, turning occasionally. Immediately place peppers in a small bowl; let stand, covered, 20 minutes. Reduce grill temperature to medium heat.

3. Grill corn and potatoes, covered, over medium heat 12-15 minutes or until tender and lightly browned, turning occasionally. Cool slightly.

4. Peel off and discard charred skin from poblanos; remove stems and seeds. Cut peppers into 1/2-in. pieces and place in a large bowl. Cut corn from cobs and cut potatoes into 3/4-in. pieces; add to peppers.

5. In a small bowl, whisk buttermilk, sour cream and lime juice until blended; stir in jalapeno, cilantro and seasonings. Add to potato mixture, stirring in as much dressing as desired to coat. Serve with lime wedges. Refrigerate leftovers.

Spicy Grilled Eggplant

INGREDIENTS

» 2 small eggplants, cut into 1/2-inch slices

» 1/4 cup olive oil

» 2 tablespoons lime juice

» 3 teaspoons Cajun seasoning

DIRECTIONS

1. Brush eggplant slices with oil. Drizzle with lime juice; sprinkle with Cajun seasoning. Let stand 5 minutes.

2. Grill eggplant, covered, over medium heat or broil 4 in. from heat until tender, 4-5 minutes per side.

Grilled Apple Tossed Salad

INGREDIENTS

» 6 tablespoons olive oil

» 1/4 cup minced fresh cilantro

» 1/4 cup orange juice

» 1/4 cup white or regular balsamic vinegar

» 2 tablespoons honey

» 1 garlic clove, minced

» 1/2 teaspoon salt

» 1/2 teaspoon Sriracha chili sauce

» 2 large apples, cut into 1/2-inch wedges

» 1 package (5 ounces) spring mix salad greens

» 1 cup walnut halves, toasted

» 1/2 cup crumbled blue cheese

DIRECTIONS

1. For dressing, whisk together first 8 ingredients. In a bowl, toss apples with 1/4 cup dressing. Let stand 10 minutes.

2. Place apple slices on a grill rack over medium heat; reserve marinade left in bowl. Grill apples, covered, until tender and lightly browned, 3-4 minutes per side, brushing with reserved marinade.

3. To serve, toss greens with remaining dressing. Top with grilled apples, walnuts and cheese.

Grilled Steak and Mushroom Salad

INGREDIENTS

- » 6 tablespoons olive oil, divided
- » 2 tablespoons Dijon mustard, divided
- » 1/2 teaspoon salt
- » 1/4 teaspoon pepper
- » 1 beef top sirloin steak (1-1/2 pounds)
- » 1 pound sliced fresh mushrooms
- » 1/4 cup red wine vinegar
- » 1 medium bunch romaine, torn

DIRECTIONS

1. In a small bowl, whisk 1 tablespoon oil, 1 tablespoon mustard, salt and pepper; set aside.

2. Grill steak, covered, over medium-hot heat for 4 minutes. Turn; spread with mustard mixture. Grill 4 minutes longer or until meat reaches desired doneness (for medium-rare, a thermometer should read 135°; medium, 140°; medium-well, 145°).

3. Meanwhile, in a large skillet, cook mushrooms in 1 tablespoon oil until tender. Stir in the vinegar and the remaining oil and mustard.

4. Thinly slice steak across the grain; add to mushroom mixture.

5. Serve over romaine.

Bratwurst Supper

INGREDIENTS

» 3 pounds uncooked bratwurst links

» 3 pounds small red potatoes, cut into wedges

» 1 pound baby carrots

» 1 large red onion, sliced and separated into rings

» 2 jars (4-1/2 ounces each) whole mushrooms, drained

» 1/4 cup butter, cubed

» 1 envelope onion soup mix

» 2 tablespoons soy sauce

» 1/2 teaspoon pepper

DIRECTIONS

1. For each of 2 foil packets, arrange a double thickness of heavy-duty foil (about 17x15 in.) on a flat surface.

2. Cut brats into thirds. Divide the brats, potatoes, carrots, onion and mushrooms evenly between the 2 double-layer foil rectangles. Dot with butter. Sprinkle with soup mix, soy sauce and pepper. Bring edges of foil together; crimp to seal, forming 2 large packets. Seal tightly; turn to coat.

3. Grill, covered, over medium heat for 23-28 minutes on each side or until vegetables are tender and sausage is no longer pink. Open foil carefully to allow steam to escape.

Fruit 'n' Cake Kabobs

INGREDIENTS

» 1/2 cup apricot preserves

» 1 tablespoon water

» 1 tablespoon butter

» 1/8 teaspoon ground cinnamon

» 1/8 teaspoon ground nutmeg

» 3 medium nectarines, quartered

» 3 medium peaches, quartered

» 3 medium plums, quartered

» 1 loaf (10-3/4 ounces) frozen pound cake, thawed and cut into 1-1/2-inch cubes

DIRECTIONS

1. In a small saucepan, combine first five ingredients; cook and stir over medium heat until blended. Remove from heat.

2. On eight metal or soaked wooden skewers, alternately thread fruit and pound cake. Place on a greased rack over medium heat. Grill, uncovered, until lightly browned and fruit is tender, brushing occasionally with apricot mixture.

Burger Americana

Total Timer Prep/Total Time: 25 min.   Servings: 4

INGREDIENTS

» 1/2 cup seasoned bread crumbs

» 1 large egg, lightly beaten

» 1/2 teaspoon salt

» 1/2 teaspoon pepper

» 1 pound ground beef

» 1 tablespoon olive oil

» 4 sesame seed hamburger buns, split

» Toppings of your choice

DIRECTIONS

1. In a large bowl, combine bread crumbs, egg, salt and pepper. Add beef; mix lightly but thoroughly. Shape into four 1/2-in.-thick patties. Press a shallow indentation in the center of each patty with your thumb. Brush both sides of patties with oil.

2. Grill burgers, covered, over medium heat or broil 4 in. from heat 4-5 minutes on each side or until a thermometer reads 160°. Serve on buns with toppings.

Grilled Salmon Packets

INGREDIENTS

» 4 salmon steaks (6 ounces each)

» 1 teaspoon lemon-pepper seasoning

» 1 cup shredded carrots

» 1/2 cup julienned sweet yellow pepper

» 1/2 cup julienned green pepper

» 4 teaspoons lemon juice

» 1 teaspoon dried parsley flakes

» 1/2 teaspoon salt

» 1/4 teaspoon pepper

DIRECTIONS

1. Sprinkle salmon with lemon-pepper. Place each salmon steak on a double thickness of heavy-duty foil (about 12 in. square). Top with carrots and peppers. Sprinkle with remaining ingredients.

2. Fold foil around fish and seal tightly. Grill, covered, over medium heat for 15-20 minutes or until fish flakes easily with a fork.

Grilled Loaded Potato Rounds

INGREDIENTS

» 4 large potatoes, baked and cooled

» 1/4 cup butter, melted

» 1/4 teaspoon salt

» 1/4 teaspoon pepper

» 1 cup sour cream

» 1-1/2 cups shredded cheddar cheese

» 8 bacon strips, cooked and crumbled

» 3 tablespoons minced chives

DIRECTIONS

1. Trim ends of potatoes. Slice potatoes into 1-in.-thick rounds. Brush with butter; sprinkle with salt and pepper. Place potatoes on grill rack, buttered side down. Grill, covered, over medium heat or broil 4 in. from heat until browned, 5-7 minutes. Brush with remaining butter; turn. Grill or broil until browned, 5-7 minutes longer.

2. Top with sour cream, cheese, bacon and chives.

Printed in the USA
CPSIA information can be obtained
at www.ICGtesting.com
LVHW011243150923
758204LV00012B/1278